STUDYING AMERICA PAST AND PRESENT

Volume II From 1865

to accompany

Divine • Breen • Fredrickson • Williams

AMERICA PAST AND PRESENT

Fourth Edition

CONTENTS

Chapter 16	The Agony of Reconstruction	1
Chapter 17	The West: Exploiting an Empire	12
Chapter 18	The Industrial Society	23
Chapter 19	Toward an Urban Society: 1877–1900	34
Chapter 20	Political Realignments in the 1890s	45
Chapter 21	Toward Empire	57
Chapter 22	The Progressive Era	68
Chapter 23	From Roosevelt to Wilson in the Age of Progressivism	80
Chapter 24	The Nation at War	93
Chapter 25	Transition to Modern America	106
Chapter 26	Franklin D. Roosevelt and the New Deal	116
Chapter 27	America and the World, 1921-1945	127
Chapter 28	Truman and the Cold War	138
Chapter 29	Affluence and Anxiety: From the Fair Deal to the Great Society	150
Chapter 30	Vietnam and the Escalating Cold War, 1953–1968	163
Chapter 31	A Crisis in Confidence, 1965–1980	174
Chapter 32	The Reagan–Bush Era	187
Chapter 33	America in Flux, 1970–1993	198
Answer Key		210

PREFACE

Our goal in writing this study guide is to make your study of American history, using *America Past and Present*, Fourth Edition, more effective and rewarding. We hope that *Studying American Past and Present* will help you

- develop the study skills you need to learn history inside and outside the classroom.
- master the text material and demonstrate your knowledge on tests and quizzes.
- develop a clear understanding of the main trends and recurring themes within American history.
- develop map-reading skills and expand your understanding of the relationship between geography and history.

To achieve these goals, we have gathered an assortment of study tips, exercises that require factual answers, and broader "thought questions"—all of which should help enhance your knowledge of the text and America history. These study aids can be divided into two general classes: essays and review exercises designed to improve your study skills and chapter-by-chapter review materials.

REVIEWING THE TEST CHAPTER BY CHAPTER

Each chapter in *Studying America Past and Present* corresponds to a chapter in your text. Each chapter of review materials includes a chapter summary, learning objectives, glossary of terms, and self-test questions that include identification, matching, completion, true/false, multiple choice, and thought questions.

- The *Summary*, which is organized around the heads and subheads within the chapter, highlights the most important points and will help you review your reading of the chapter.

- The *Learning Objectives* pinpoint the most important themes or ideas of the chapter, themes and ideas you should take away from your study. Refer back to this list as you review the text chapter and as you complete the self-test exercises to see how well you have mastered the material.

- The *Glossary* contains a number of terms that may be unfamiliar to you. Besides a definition, we have supplied a quote from the chapter that shows you how the word can be used in a sentence. Learning these words and terms will expand your vocabulary, which will help you in this and other courses in the social sciences.

- The *self-test exercises* cover both specific details and broad concepts. (An answer key for these questions is at the end of the text). *Identification* items ask you to identify key phrases and explain their significance. *Matching* exercises are intended to help you distinguish between similar but different people, locations, or events. By asking you to fill in the blanks, *Completion* exercises will help you relate specific items to their context. *True/False* and *Multiple Choice* questions will give you valuable practice for objective tests and help you check your knowledge of key points.

- *Thought Questions* are designed to meet the objective of helping you develop a clear understanding of the main trends and recurring themes within American history. Answering these questions will help you tie together your classroom lecture notes and the text coverage; this will also help you study for essay tests, a feature of most history courses.

For best results, try to use the chapter-by-chapter review materials in a consistent manner. Read the chapter and then begin working through the chapter's review materials, using the "Summary" and "Learning Objectives" to focus your study. After you have completed the self-test exercises, check your answers against the answer key. When you understand why you missed a question and determine areas of weakness, focus your attention on reviewing those sections. If you do this faithfully, both your knowledge and pleasure in American history should increase. We hope you find your efforts worthwhile and your confidence in your ability to learn and enjoy history enhanced. If so, we will have accomplished our goals.

The Authors

CHAPTER 16

THE AGONY OF RECONSTRUCTION

SUMMARY
After the Civil War, the South faced a difficult period of rebuilding its government and economy and of dealing with the newly freed African Americans.

THE PRESIDENT VERSUS CONGRESS
In the absence of constitutional guidelines, the president and Congress waged a bitter fight over how best to reconstruct the Union.

Wartime Reconstruction
By 1863, Lincoln and Congress had begun to debate two divisive issues: the reconstruction of the southern states and the status of the freedmen. Lincoln proposed a minimal program to restore the southern states to the Union and showed some willingness to compromise with Congress in the months before his death. But the Reconstruction issues remained unresolved.

Andrew Johnson at the Helm
Johnson's ascent to the presidency led to a bitter clash with Congress. There was a uniform hope of breaking the power of the planter class, but Congress supported federal guarantees for black citizenship, and Johnson insisted that the South be permitted to reestablish white supremacy.

Congress Takes the Initiative
Determined to crush the old southern ruling class, the Republican-led Congress extended the life of the Freedmen's Bureau and passed a civil rights bill to grant equal benefits and protection to the freedmen. Fearing that Johnson would not enforce the civil rights act, Congress passed the Fourteenth Amendment guaranteeing equal rights under the law to all Americans and defining national citizenship. After the southern states rejected the amendment, and the president vetoed two Reconstruction bills, Congress initiated its own radical program.

CONGRESSIONAL RECONSTRUCTION PLAN ENACTED
The First Reconstruction Act of 1867 temporarily placed the South under military rule and allowed for the readmittance of southern states once African American suffrage was legitimized.

The Impeachment Crisis
When the president obstructed the plan's implementation, Congress retaliated with an attempt to remove him from office. Johnson narrowly avoided removal, preserving the office from

congressional domination, but insuring also that Congress would have the upper hand in the reconstruction process.

RECONSTRUCTION IN THE SOUTH
The South was devastated and demoralized after the war, and dominated by southern whites who wanted to deny all rights to freedmen.

Social and Economic Adjustments
When Congress failed to enact a program of land redistribution, southern landowners initiated a new labor system that forced freedmen into virtual peonage. Most of the ex-slaves had no alternative but to return to white-owned fields under a contract labor system. While sharecropping extended black servitude and economic dependence on the farm, segregation of the races was imposed in the towns.

Political Reconstruction in the South
Politically, Reconstruction established southern governments of Republican businesspeople, poor whites, and freedmen. Although often corrupt, these radical regimes initiated significant progressive reforms. They failed however to achieve interracial equality; community pressure established a social system based on segregation.

THE AGE OF GRANT
Serving during one of the most difficult periods in American history, Grant lacked the strong principles, consistency, and sense of purpose to be an effective administrator.

Rise of the Money Question
What to do with the greenbacks (paper money issued during the war) became a major problem by 1868. Hard money advocates clashed with "greenbackers" who wanted government-sponsored inflation. The panic of 1873 intensified the argument, and the Sherman Specie Resumption Act in 1874 failed to please either the inflationists or the hard-money advocates.

Retreat from Reconstruction
In the South, Grant's administration failed to sustain black suffrage against violent groups bent on restoring white supremacy. Organizations like the Ku Klux Klan used terrorism, insurrection, and murder to intimidate southern Republican governments and prospective black voters. With the Fifteenth Amendment severely threatened, Congress passed the "Force" Acts which allowed the president to use military force to quell insurrections.

Spoilsmen versus Reformers
The idealism of radical republicanism waned as new leaders—"spoilsmen"—came to power determined to further their own private interests. The Crédit Mobilier scandal, the "Whiskey Ring," and the impeachment of Secretary of War Belknap for accepting bribes left liberal reform Republicans aghast and the Grant administration in shambles.

REUNION AND THE NEW SOUTH
The reconciliation of the sections came at the expense of southern blacks and poor whites.

The Compromise of 1877
In the 1876 presidential election, Samuel Tilden, the Democratic candidate, won the popular majority as well as the uncontested electoral vote. But disputed returns in the three Republican-controlled southern states threw the election into turmoil. The Compromise of 1877 ended military rule and insured that conservative "home rule" would be restored in the South. With southern Democratic acquiescence, Republican candidate Rutherford Hayes assumed the presidency.

The New South
In the South, upper-class "Redeemers" took power in the name of white supremacy and industrial development and then initiated a "New South." The economy was dominated by northern capital and southern employers, landlords, and creditors. Economic and physical coercion, including hundreds of lynchings, effectively disenfranchised people of color. Some blacks, justifiably bitter at the depth of white racism, supported black nationalism and emigration to Africa, but most chose to struggle for improvement within American society.

LEARNING OBJECTIVES

After mastering this chapter, you should be able to

1. Contrast the presidential and congressional wartime reconstruction programs.

2. Explain how Andrew Johnson's background shaped his attitudes and policies on Reconstruction.

3. Describe the processes by which Andrew Johnson lost support in Congress and the Radical Republicans gained control of Reconstruction.

4. Summarize the goals of Radical Reconstruction and evaluate the success with which these goals were achieved.

5. Define the sections of the Fourteenth Amendment and understand why its enforcement was crucial to Reconstruction efforts.

6. Describe the Radicals' attempt to remove President Johnson from office.

7. Define the southern systems of contract labor and sharecropping with emphasis on their effects upon African Americans.

8. Evaluate Grant's handling of the major problems of his administration: the money question, enforcement of Reconstruction, and governmental corruption.

9. Analyze the important results of the impeachment crisis on the federal government and the Reconstruction process.

10. Identify the social and economic adjustments in the South during the Reconstruction years.

11. Evaluate the achievements and list reasons for the ultimate failure of the southern Republican governments.

12. Summarize the worst of the scandals which rocked the Grant administration.

13. Explain the nature of the political crisis involving the election of 1876.

14. Discuss the terms and results of the Compromise of 1877.

15. Describe the social and political effects of the "Redeemer" regimes in the New South.

GLOSSARY

To build your social science vocabulary, familiarize yourself with the following terms:

1. **crop lien** use of a farmer's crop as collateral for a loan. ". . . the notorious 'crop lien' system. . . ."

2. **disfranchisement** the act of depriving a citizen of the right to vote. "Full-scale disfranchisement. . . ."

3. **impeachment** the act of bringing charges against a government officer for official misconduct. ". . . to call for his impeachment."

4. **Jim Crow** segregated. ". . black, or 'Jim Crow,' cars. . . ."

5. **laissez-faire** government noninterference in the economy. ". . . advocated strict laissez-faire economic policies. . . ."

6. **patronage** political control of the distribution of jobs and other favors. ". . . the corruption-breeding patronage system. . . ."

7. **referendum** the practice of referring a matter to the electorate for adoption or rejection. ". . . served as a referendum to the Fourteenth Amendment."

8. **specie** coined money, usually of gold or silver. ". . . redeemed in specie payments."

9. **amnesty** a pardon granted for past crimes. ". . . a Proclamation of Amnesty and Reconstruction. . . ."

10. **habeas corpus** a legal writ used to protect individuals against unlawful detention. ". . . suspend the writ of habeas corpus. . ."

11. **rider** a clause added to a bill as it passes a legislative body. ". . . a rider to an army appropriations bill—sought to limit Johnson's authority to issue orders to military commanders."

12. **revisionism** proposing a revised historical interpretation. "The most powerful example of this early revisionism was W.E.B. Dubois' *Black Reconstruction in America*."

13. **provisional** temporary, until a permanent replacement is made. ". . . appointed provisional governors. . . ."

14. **sharecropping** the status of working a piece of land in return for a portion of the crop. ". . . an alternative capital-labor relationship—sharecropping. . ."

15. **autonomy** the right and power of self-government. "The president's case for state autonomy. . . ."

IDENTIFICATION

Briefly identify the meaning and significance of the following terms.

1. Jim Crow _____

_____

2. Wade-Davis bill _____

_____

3. Freedmen's Bureau _____

_____

4. Fourteenth Amendment _____

_____

5. Thaddeus Stevens _____
_____

6. First Reconstruction Act _____
_____

7. "carpetbaggers" _____
_____

8. John Sherman _____
_____

9. Horace Greeley _____
_____

10. New South _____
_____

MATCHING

A. Match the following public figures with the appropriate description.

_____ 1. Orville Babcock
_____ 2. William Belknap
_____ 3. Schuyler Colfax
_____ 4. Jay Gould
_____ 5. Carl Schurz

a. secretary of war who resigned to prevent a Senate trial for taking bribes in the sale of Indian trading posts

b. senator from Missouri who helped lead the crusade for civil service reform

c. president's private secretary who was indicted for his role in the "Whiskey Ring"

d. Speaker of the House and later vice-president who was implicated in the Crédit Mobilier scandal

e. financier who, with the help of a relative of the president, tried to corner the gold market

f. New York City "boss" who headed a corrupt Democratic political "machine"

B. Match the following bills and acts with the appropriate description.

_____1. Wade-Davis bill
a. congressional legislation designed to limit the authority of President Andrew Johnson

_____2. Black Codes
b. a series of laws designed to protect black suffrage by authorizing use of the army against the KKK

_____3. Tenure of Office Act
c. initial congressional plan for Reconstruction vetoed by Lincoln

_____4. Force Acts
d. congressional attempt to provide the freedman "full and equal benefit" of all laws

_____5. Civil Rights Bill of 1866
e. southern state laws passed during Reconstruction to impose restrictions on former slaves

f. congressional legislation creating a federal agency to aid former slaves

COMPLETION

Answer the question or complete the statement by filling in the blanks with the correct word or words.

1. The 1915 epic film of D. W. Griffith that presented Reconstruction as a "tragic era" of misrule and corruption was entitled _____.

2. Slavery was abolished with the ratification of the _____.

3. Lincoln refused to sign the Wade-Davis bill of 1864 by exercising a _____.

4. The physical destruction of the South would not have been so devastating had there been sufficient _____ available for rebuilding.

5. The _____ Amendment restricted the power of the Fourteenth states to violate the life, liberty, or property of any citizen.

6. By the 1870s, most African Americans were relegated to the position of _____, an arrangement whereby they agreed to work a small piece of land in return for a fixed share of the crop.

7. In 1874, President Grant discouraged inflation by vetoing a modest new issue of _____.

8. The _____ was a southern society bent on restoring white supremacy by intimidating politically active African Americans.

9. The southern Republican party consisted of the following three groups _____.

10. By the 1870s, leadership of the Republican party had passed to opportunistic politicians called _____, who were more interested in personal gain than in public service.

TRUE/FALSE

Mark the following statements either T (True) or F (False).

_____ 1. Lincoln favored a lenient plan for Reconstruction in order to shorten the war by attracting southern support.

_____ 2. The dominant view of the Republican-led Congress toward the Reconstruction process was that strong executive leadership would be required.

_____ 3. Andrew Johnson abandoned Lincoln's plans for Reconstruction by doing away with the requirement of an oath of allegiance for southern whites.

_____ 4. Women's rights leaders Elizabeth Cady Stanton and Susan B. Anthony campaigned against ratification of the Fifteenth Amendment.

_____ 5. As a result of his impeachment trial, Andrew Johnson became the first president to be removed from office.

_____ 6. Physical reconstruction of the South was difficult because its per capita wealth in 1865 was only about half of what it had been in 1860.

_____ 7. The "Greenbackers" in the credit-hungry West favored sound money policies.

_____ 8. The Fifteenth Amendment to the Constitution prohibited any state from denying any citizen the right to vote because of race, color, or previous condition of servitude.

_____ 9. During Grant's first term, the greatest threat to southern Republican governments came from white supremist societies like the Ku Klux Klan.

_____10. The factor which most contributed to Democrat Samuel Tilden's defeat in the presidential election in 1876 was the continued strength of the Republican regimes in the South and his consequent lack of popular support there.

MULTIPLE CHOICE

Circle the one alternative that *best* completes the statement or answers the question.
1. Which of the following statements reflects Lincoln's view of Reconstruction?
    a. Amnesty would be granted to those Southerners who had never willingly aided the Confederacy.
    b. Reconstruction would guarantee full political and civil equality for southern blacks.
    c. Congress would determine the terms for readmission of the seceded states.
    d. Pardon would be granted to all Southerners taking an oath of allegiance to the Union and acknowledging the legality of emancipation.

2. President Andrew Johnson's plan for Reconstruction called for the southern states to
    a. declare their ordinances of secession illegal.
    b. repay their Confederate war debts.
    c. ratify the Fourteenth Amendment.
    d. prohibit former Confederates from holding government offices.

3. The Fourteenth Amendment to the Constitution
    a. prohibited slavery in the United States.
    b. provided for franchise regardless of race, color, or past servitude.
    c. defined national citizenship and prohibited the states from abridging the constitutional rights of people without due process of law.
    d. restored the former slave states to the Union after congressional requirements were met.

4. President Johnson antagonized Republicans in Congress by
    a. calling for an extension of the Freedmen's Bureau.
    b. supporting a civil rights bill meant to guarantee equality for African Americans.
    c. urging confiscation and redistribution of land.
    d. campaigning against Radical Republicans in the elections of 1866.

5. After rejecting Johnson's Reconstruction plan, Congress enacted a program based on
    a. the social and moral regeneration of the South.
    b. the confiscation and redistribution of land.
    c. immediate enfranchisement of both the freedmen and ex-Confederates.
    d. guarantees for the rights of all citizens with the Fourteenth Amendment.

6. The House of Representatives impeached President Johnson on the grounds that he
   a. dismissed officers in the southern military districts.
   b. challenged the Tenure of Office Act by removing Secretary of War Edwin Stanton.
   c. vetoed the Reconstruction bill.
   d. attempted to abolish the Freedmen's Bureau.

7. "Regeneration before Reconstruction" referred to
   a. restructuring southern state governments before readmission to the union.
   b. funding the rehabilitation of those areas in the South damaged during the war.
   c. transforming southern society, including land reform to the freedmen, before readmission.
   d. repudiating the debts owed by the former Confederate states to the Union.

8. Hard-money proponents favored
   a. more money in circulation to spur economic growth.
   b. retirement of greenbacks as quickly as possible and payment in silver and gold only.
   c. redemption of much of the war debt in greenbacks.
   d. easy credit terms to encourage economic expansion in the West.

9. Farmers and debtors generally favored a monetary policy that
   a. expanded the currency and inflated prices.
   b. contracted the currency and deflated prices.
   c. legally backed all currency with gold only.
   d. kept commodity prices stable and dependable.

10. The main reason[s] for the Ku Klux Klan's success in the South after 1868 was
    a. popular support from whites of all social classes for white supremacy.
    b. its centralized political organization.
    c. its support from the southern state Republican governments.
    d. the persistent threat of a violent black uprising against the white planter class.

11. The three social groups which formed the coalition of the southern Republican party were
    a. businesspeople, poor white farmers, and former slaves.
    b. wealthy planters, professionals, and urban laborers.
    c. urban middle class, independent small farmers, and carpetbaggers.
    d. white agricultural laborers, wealthy businessmen, and black sharecroppers.

12. In defending Republican governments in the South, President Grant
    a. was quick to react with the military to any threat of violence.
    b. intervened only to protect the civil rights of African Americans.
    c. was inconsistent and hesitant because of northern political realities.
    d. left these governments on their own to defend themselves.

13. How would you characterize Grant's personal role in the corruption that marked his administration?
    a. He should be considered completely blameless.
    b. He vigorously prosecuted all wrongdoing.
    c. He protected some corrupt officials from justice.
    d. He made a great deal of money from illegal activities.

14. To ensure the election of Rutherford Hayes, Republican leaders agreed to
    a. offer lucrative positions to members of the electoral commission.
    b. end federal support for southern radical regimes.
    c. support fraudulent elections with federal troops.
    d. continue federal support for southern radical regimes.

15. The "Redeemers" in the South favored
    a. egalitarian democracy and continued Republican leadership.
    b. government appropriations for schools and public services and economic diversification.
    c. strengthening the Black Codes and support for white supremacist organizations like the Klan.
    d. political restoration of white supremacy and the gospel of industrial progress.

THOUGHT QUESTIONS

To check your understanding of the key issues of this period, solve the following problems:

1. If Lincoln had lived, would the events and outcome of Reconstruction have been substantially different?

2. Was radical Reconstruction policy based more on humanitarian concern for the freedmen or on selfish political and economic interests?

3. Andrew Johnson was the only U.S. president impeached in our history. (Richard M. Nixon tendered a timely resignation.) What does it mean to impeach a president? Should Andrew Johnson have been convicted?

4. What factors contributed to the development of segregation in the late nineteenth century?

5. Government plays a role in determining the supply of money and, therefore, general price levels. During Grant's administration what factors led the president to allow special interests to determine his policy on the money question?

6. Why did most professional historians from the 1890s to the 1940s regard Reconstruction as a "tragic era"? In the eyes of the revisionists, what was the real tragedy of Reconstruction?

CHAPTER 17

THE WEST: EXPLOITING AN EMPIRE

SUMMARY
After the War, Americans, believing expansion was their "manifest destiny," created a great colonial empire in the West.

BEYOND THE FRONTIER
Prior to the Civil War, the march of Anglo settlement paused at the margin of the semiarid Great Plains, a temporary obstacle to further migration.

CRUSHING THE NATIVE AMERICANS
Because they were an additional obstacle to further white migration, the Native Americans lost their lands and and radically changed their cultures by the end of the century.

Life of the Plains Indians

After they acquired the Spanish horse, the Plains Indians abandoned their former lifestyle in favor of a strong, unique culture based upon the buffalo.

"As Long as Waters Run"

Earlier in the century, the Great Plains, known as the Great American Desert, was considered by the United States government as unusable for whites and was given to the Native Americans. But with the discovery of gold in the West, the federal government began a policy of restricting tribes to reservations. This new policy led to conflicts with the Native Americans.

Final Battles on the Plains

From 1867 to 1890, the federal government fought a number of tribes in brutal campaigns, eliminating any semblance of resistance.

The End of Tribal Life

In 1887, Congress began a policy of ending tribal life and turning the Native Americans into farmers. Still another crushing blow to the traditional tribal ways occurred when white hunters nearly exterminated the buffalo.

SETTLEMENT OF THE WEST
In the last three decades of the nineteenth century, Anglo farmers brought more land under the plow in America than ever before.

Men and Women on the Overland Trail
Settlers flocked to the west. In the three decades after the Gold Rush of 1849, some one-half million individuals traveled the Overland Trail westward across half a continent in search of riches, adventure, and a healthier life.

Land for the Taking
Government policy provided free or cheap land to individual settlers, land speculators, and private corporations such as the railroads, all eager to supply the needs of a growing nation for the products of the West.

Territorial Government
The new territories of the West related to the government like colonies.

The Spanish-Speaking Southwest
The Spanish-Mexican heritage of the Southwest gave a distinctive shape to that area's politics, language, society, and law.

THE BONANZA WEST
Quests for quick profits led to a boom-bust cycle in the western economy.

The Mining Bonanza
Lured by the prospect of mineral wealth throughout the region, many settlers moved west, building hasty and often short-lived communities, which reflected primarily materialistic and exploitative interests.

Gold from the Roots Up
Large profits also were possible for the cattle ranchers who grazed their herds on the prairie grasses and drove them to the railheads.

FARMING ON THE FRONTIER
Millions of pioneer farmers settled the West by 1900.

Sodbusters on the Plains
They were led by the sodbusters, or the dirt farmers, who slowly moved out onto the Great Plains where they encountered enormous obstacles.

New Farming Methods
Several important inventions, innovations, and adaptations made farming on the treeless, semiarid Plains possible.

Discontent on the Farm
Bad weather and low prices stirred up the farmers' anger, leading some to form political lobbies, andothers to adopt more scientific, businesslike methods.

The Final Fling

The Oklahoma land rush of 1889 symbolized the closing of the frontier and in many ways reflected the attitude of Anglo-Americans toward Native Americans and their land.

LEARNING OBJECTIVES

After mastering this chapter, you should be able to

1. Describe the geographic and climatic conditions of the four major regions of settlement between Missouri and the Pacific.

2. Distinguish the basic cultural features of the Pueblo, Plains, California, and Northwestern tribes.

3. Analyze the factors that ended tribal life for the Native Americans.

4. Explain the United States policies toward Native Americans and the results of those policies.

5. Discuss the motives that stimulated settlement of the West.

6. Describe the journey along the Overland Trail.

7. List and explain the land laws passed by the federal government in the latter half of the nineteenth century.

8. Locate the mineral strikes of the West and describe the life that developed in the mining camps.

9. Trace the boom-and-bust development of the open-range cattle industry.

10. Describe the problems faced by early farmers of the Great Plains and the new methods with which they addressed their problems.

GLOSSARY

To build your social science vocabulary, familiarize yourself with the following terms:

1. **communal** shared in common by all members of a group. ". . . they built communal houses. . . ."

2. **nomadic** relating to a culture or tribe that moves about in search of food or pasturage. "Nomadic and warlike, the Plains Indians. . . ."

3. **migratory** roving or wandering from place to place, usually in response to seasonal changes. "Migratory in culture. . . ."

4. **assimilate** to make similar, alike, or to bring into conformity with. ". . . urging instead that the nation assimilate them individually into white culture. . . ."

5. **internment** the state of being jailed or confined. " 'Except for the internment of the West Coast Japanese. . . .' "

6. **speculators** buyers or sellers who expect to profit from market fluctuations. "Speculators made ingenious use of the land laws."

7. **mandate** a territory over which another nation assumes authority and responsibility for establishment of government. "Washington ran the territories like 'a passive group of colonial mandates'."

8. **patronage** the awarding of government jobs on a basis other than merit (i.e., friendship, financial support, etc.). "[The territories] became an important part of the patronage system. . . ."

9. **placer mining** surface mining in which gravels are picked or dredged from deposits; ore is separated from the wastes by panning or sluicing. ". . . they used a simple process called placer mining."

10. **simple democracy** uncomplicated rules and penalties characteristic of the government of early mining towns. "Mining camps were governed by a simple democracy."

11. **banished** ordered by authorities to leave a geographic area. "Petty criminals were banished from the district."

12. **absentee owner** a landowner who does not live on or directly work the land he or she owns. ". . . often controlled by absentee owners and subject to new problems. . . ."

13. **aborigines** the original people or inhabitants of a region or country. ". . . 'wandering and uncivilized aborigines.' "

14. **sodbusters** Great Plains farmers who first broke the sod made up of the roots of the tough prairie grasses. "Sodbusters on the Plains."

15. **Sooner** settler who moved onto government land before it was officially open, hence, a nickname for an Oklahoman. ". . . 'Sooners'—those who had jumped the gun. . . ."

IDENTIFICATION

Briefly identify the meaning and significance of the following terms.

1. Great Plains _____
   _____

2. Wounded Knee _____
   _____

3. Dawes Severalty Act _____
   _____

4. Overland Trail _____
   _____

5. Homestead Act of 1862 _____
   _____

6. Las Gorras Blancas _____
   _____

7. Comstock Lode _____
   _____

8. Chinese Exclusion Act _____
   _____

9. Chisholm Trail _____
   _____

MATCHING

A. Match the following leaders with the appropriate description.

_____1. Black Kettle

a. Sioux chief who ambushed Captain William J. Fetterman in response to the government's plans to build the Bozeman Trail

_____2. Red Cloud

b. leader of the Cheyenne during the merciless massacre by Colonel John M. Chivington at Sand Creek

_____3. Chief Joseph

c. Nez Percé chief who led his tribe on a phenomenal flight to Canada in 1877

_____4. Crazy Horse

d. War Chief of the Sioux who led them in battle against Lieutenant Colonel George A. Custer at the Little Big Horn

_____5. Sitting Bull

e. spiritual leader of Sioux in the campaign against whites in 1875–1876

f. aging leader of Teton Sioux in the time of the Ghost Dance religion and the massacre at Wounded Knee

B. Match the following individuals with the appropriate description.

_____1. Horace Greeley

a. early explorer who thought the land west of the Mississippi uninhabitable for whites

_____2. Samuel Johnson

b. historian who wrote that the frontier shaped American character

_____3. Oliver Dalrymple

c. editor who urged unemployed readers to settle western farms

_____4. Oliver Kelley

d. Yale professor who wrote books on crop growth and soil minerals

_____5. Frederick Jackson Turner

e. bonanza farmer who produced 600,000 bushels of wheat in one year

f. government clerk who founded organizations to provide farmers with social, cultural, and educational activities

COMPLETION

Answer the question or complete the statement by filling in the blanks with the correct word or words.

1. Historian Walter Prescott Webb argued that the Great Plains lacked two of the three "legs" on which Eastern civilization had stood. The three legs were _____, _____, and _____.

2. The Paiute messiah who had a vision that Indians would gain a new life if they performed the "Ghost Dances" was named _____.

3. The Plains Indians developed a nomadic life style, hunting, and living off every part of the _____.

4. One of the most famous professional buffalo hunters and the producer of a "Wild West" show was _____.

5. Most wagon trains bound for the West began their journey at _____.

6. To lure land-seeking Europeans to the American West, railroads set up _____ of _____.

7. The idea of shipping cattle to Chicago by railroad belonged to Joseph G. _____.

8. At each mining site, individual prospectors first removed surface ore by using simple _____.

9. Farmers on the Plains compensated for the lack of water with a technique called _____.

10. Agricultural extension stations, which helped spread new techniques to American farmers, were supported by _____ Act of 1877.

TRUE/FALSE

Mark the following statements either T (True) or F (False).

_____1. Westerners created subsistence economies that were largely independent of both eastern capital and the federal government.

_____2. The material culture of the Plains Indians was based on a diversity of animal and plant life.

_____3. United States policy toward Native Americans aimed at maintaining tribal life.

_____4. Red Cloud's victories caused the government to change policy and attempt to "civilize" Native American tribes.

_____5. Americans settled more land between 1870 and 1900 than in all the years before 1870.

_____6. Government officials made sure that only legitimate farming families received any of the federal lands.

_____7. The Spanish-Mexican heritage of the Southwest had important impact on the development of that region.

_____8. The mining and cattle industries experienced a slow but steady growth pattern in the decades after the Civil War.

_____9. The Great Plains area was a problem for Anglo settlers because of Native American tribes, the relative scarcity of trees, and the inadequacy of rainfall.

_____10. The droughts of the 1880s slowed the march of the pioneer Anglo farmers.

MULTIPLE CHOICE

Circle the one alternative that *best* completes the statement or answers the question.

1. Early explorers thought the trans-Mississippi West best suited for
   a. irrigated farmland.
   b. ranching grassland.
   c. timber and minerals.
   d. Indians and buffalo.

2. The Plains Indians were
   a. organized into one large and powerful tribal group.
   b. an insignificant proportion of the total Native American population in the United States in 1870.
   c. a complex of tribes, cultures, and bands that assigned most work on the basis of sex.
   d. at a distinct disadvantage when fighting whites because of weapons.

3. Government policy toward Native Americans
   a. ignored or opposed tribal organization.
   b. was consistent but not successful because of tribal organization.
   c. was formulated by the eastern humanitarians who wanted to preserve tribal organization.
   d. was a failure because the Indians insisted on being farmers.

4. All of the following were problems for the pioneer farmers of the Great Plains *except*
   a. lack of rain.
   b. declining crop prices.
   c. lack of available land.
   d. inadequate housing materials.

5. By the 1700s, the culture of the Plains Indians had been revolutionized by
   a. reservation life.
   b. new farming techniques.
   c. the Pueblo Indians.
   d. the introduction of the European horse.

6. The Dawes Severalty Act of 1887
   a. gave small plots of reservation lands to individual Native Americans.
   b. succeeded because it respected tribal organization.
   c. placed power in the hands of the Indians' traditional leaders or chiefs.
   d. prevented the alienation of Indian leaders.

7. Between 1870 and 1900, most settlers moved west to
   a. seek freedom from religious persecution.
   b. escape the drab routine of factory life.
   c. escape the diseased conditions of crowded eastern cities.
   d. improve their economic situation.

8. The most difficult leg of the Overland Trail was the
   a. initial journey to Fort Kearney.
   b. pass through the Rocky Mountains.
   c. barren stretch between Fort Laramie and Fort Hall.
   d. final trek through the desert and the Sierra Nevada.

9. One purpose of the Dawes Act was to
   a. separate the civilized from the uncivilized tribes.
   b. enforce all previous treaties between the federal government and the various tribes.
   c. force Native Americans to abandon communal ownership of land.
   d. support Native American religions, such as the Ghost Dance movement.

10. Between 1862 and 1890, the federal government gave more land to
    a. individual homesteaders.
    b. private corporations.
    c. railroad companies.
    d. state governments.

11. Cities like Abilene, Fort Worth, and Dodge City owed their population growth and prosperity primarily to
    a. silver mining.
    b. their location in the farming belt.
    c. shipping or receiving cattle.
    d. the discovery of oil in nearby fields.

12. The Great Plains presented "sodbusters" with one problem not faced by farmers of earlier American frontiers. It was
    a. hostile Indians.
    b. scarce water and timber.
    c. isolation and loneliness.
    d. inadequate transportation.

13. One of the results of the rapid increase in cultivated acres the latter half of the nineteenth century was
    a. higher tariffs on farm products.
    b. lower prices for farm products.
    c. a decrease in demand for farm machinery.
    d. an increase in land values.

14. The farming boom on the Plains lasted until the
    a. Panic of 1893.
    b. bumper crop of 1884.
    c. rise of the "bonanza" farms in the 1870s.
    d. droughts of 1887–1894.

15. By the Dawes Act of 1887, the Indian Bureau tried to
    a. end the traditional Native American religions and encourage Christianity among the tribes.
    b. increase the power of the tribal councils.
    c. establish Indian-controlled and -funded educational institutions.
    d. seek out urban-industrial employment for young, male Indians.

THOUGHT QUESTIONS

To check your understanding of the key issues of this period, solve the following problems:

1. Was Horace Greeley's 1867 editorial on the agrarian opportunity of the West an overly optimistic view of the conditions and forces at work on the Great Plains?

2. Why did the policy of the government toward Native Americans waver from 1834 to 1934?

3. Theodore Roosevelt once stated that the only alternative to the defeat of the Indian was to "keep the entire continent as a game preserve for squalid savages." Explain the causes and results of such an attitude.

4. Why did tribal organization conflict with Americans' view of the good life?

5. What factors propelled and made possible rapid settlement of the American West from 1870 to 1900? What were the economic and political consequences?

6. What influence did the Spanish-Mexican heritage have on the development of the American Southwest?

7. How does the popular image (or the Hollywood screen image) of the West differ from the realistic, historical view?

CHAPTER 18

THE INDUSTRIAL SOCIETY

SUMMARY
By their centennial of 1876, Americans were rapidly developing their society.

INDUSTRIAL DEVELOPMENT
Several factors contributed to the rapid economic transformation of the era: resources for materials, population for labor and markets, railroads for transportation, tariffs for protection from competition, confident investors for capital, and technology for production. The government provided grants, stability, and freedom from regulation.

AN EMPIRE ON RAILS
Revolutionary changes in transportation and communication, especially the railroads, transformed American technology.

"Emblem of Motion and Power"
By ending rural isolation, encouraging economic specialization, creating a national market, and capturing the nation's imagination, the railroads transformed production, distribution, and business practices.

Building the Empire
By the end of the century, Americans, with substantial aid from governments, had built almost 200,000 miles of track. Despite much waste and corruption, the railroads probably did more good than harm; for example, they saved the federal government $1 billion from 1850–1945.

Linking the Nation via Trunk Lines
Before the Civil War, railroad construction served local markets; after 1865 the railroads tied the nation together with a system of trunk lines, except for the South, where railroads were not consolidated and integrated into the national railroad system until the 1880s.

Rails across the Continent
Congress voted to allow two companies, the Union Pacific, working westward, and the Central Pacific, working eastward, to compete in the construction of the first transcontinental railroad. They completed the tracks in May, 1869. By 1893, four more railroad lines reached the west coast.

Problems of Growth
Overbuilding generated vigorous rate wars, but financierss like J. P. Morgan constructed regional monopolies to reduce or eliminate competition.

AN INDUSTRIAL EMPIRE
The Bessemer process made possible an industrial empire based on steel.

Carnegie and Steel
The process for manufacturing steel required much capital, so new companies grew very large until J. P. Morgan combined a number of them, including Carnegie's, into the country's first billion-dollar corporation.

Rockefeller and Oil
John D. Rockefeller ordered the chaotic oil business into a third giant; his Standard Oil trust of the 1880s, reorganized as a holding company in the 1890s, came to control over 90 percent of oil refining in America.

THE BUSINESS OF INVENTION
And finally, the business of invention boomed-from 2,000 patents per year to over 21,000 per year—and transformed the communication, food, and power industries.

THE SELLERS
Brand names, advertising, chain stores, and mail-order houses brought the new goods to households and initiated a new community of consumers.

THE WAGE EARNERS
Although their lives improved in some respects because of new goods, workers suffered grueling, dangerous jobs. Women, children, African Americans, Catholics, Jews, and immigrants carried the additional burden of discrimination.

Culture of Work
All found that the new factory system required difficult and often demeaning adaptations in age-old patterns of work. But most workers accepted the system because it offered substantial social mobility.

Labor Unions
National unions approached the problems in different ways: the Knights of Labor, for example, organized like a fraternal order and sought broad social reforms, while the American Federation of Labor organized craft unions of skilled workers and sought practical, immediate, and tangible improvements for its members.

Labor Unrest

Workers also organized social and fraternal groups to offer members companionship, insurance, job listings, and even food for the sick. Employees tried to humanize the factory while employers tried to determine wages and conditions on the basis of supply and demand rather than the welfare of the workers. The conflict of purposes led to sometimes violent strikes.

LEARNING OBJECTIVES

After mastering this chapter, you should be able to

1. Discuss each of the major factors that contributed to the rapid industrialization of 1870–1900.

2. Describe the principal economic and social effects of the railroad, 1865–1900.

3. Trace the building of the American railroad network, 1865–1900.

4. Detail the rise and consolidation of the steel industry.

5. Detail the rise and consolidation of the oil industry.

6. List and describe the most important inventions of the last third of the nineteenth century, including their major effects.

7. Identify and explain each of the major factors in the development of a national consumer market.

8. Compare the effects of industrialization on the working lives of native-born white Anglo-Saxon Protestant males and, on the other hand, women, children, Catholics, Jews, and immigrants.

9. Identify the adaptations in the "culture of work" required by the new factory system, and the response to those changes by working people.

10. Compare and contrast the policies and methods of the Knights of Labor and the American Federation of Labor.

11. Delineate the different approaches to factory conditions and wages taken by employees and employers, then describe the resulting conflicts.

GLOSSARY

To build your social science vocabulary, familiarize yourself with the following terms:

1. **entrepreneurs** those who assume the opportunities and risks for business ventures. "In this atmosphere, entrepreneurs flourished."

2. **economic specialization** the production or distribution of a specific good or service. [The railroad] ". . . encouraged economic specialization."

3. **trunk lines** major routes or channels of transportation. ". . . four great trunk lines took shape. . . ."

4. **pools** combinations of businesses for specific purposes, such as eliminating competition and raising prices. ". . . steel companies . . . tried secret agreements, pools, and consolidation."

5. **vertical integration** business combination including some of each stage of a production process. ". . . they moved toward vertical integration. . . ."

6. **philanthropy** donation of money, time, or property to the needy or to institutions helping the needy. ". . . he wanted to devote his full time to philanthropy."

7. **trust** a type of combination of businesses to reduce competition. ". . . the first of the modern trusts was born."

8. **monopoly** a company that controls an economic good or service. "The word *trust* became synonymous with monopoly. . . ."

9. **holding company** a firm that owns enough stock in another company (or companies) to control it (them). "American Telephone and Telegraph . . . became another of the vast holding companies. . . ."

10. **magnate** a person with great power and wealth. ". . . few workers became steel magnates. . . ."

11. **fraternal order** a social organization of men. "A secret fraternal order, it grew slowly."

12. **socialism** an economic system in which society owns the means of production and distribution of goods and services. ". . . he . . . experimented for a time with socialism. . . ."

13. **injunction** a judicial order commanding a person or corporation to do, or to refrain from doing, a particular act. "The injunction . . . was used to break the great Pullman strike."

14. **armories** sites for making, repairing, or storing weapons. "Cities strengthened their armories."

15. **anarchism** the doctrine that all governments oppress individuals and should be abolished. "Linking labor and anarchism in the public mind. . . ."

IDENTIFICATION

Briefly identify the meaning and significance of the following terms.

1. Centennial Exposition _____

_____

2. Central and Union Pacific Railroad Companies _____

_____

3. J. P. Morgan _____

_____

4. Andrew Carnegie _____

_____

5. John D. Rockefeller _____

_____

6. National Labor Union _____

_____

7. Knights of Labor _____

_____

8. American Federation of Labor _____

_____

9. Thomas Alva Edison _____

_____

10. trunk lines _____

_____

MATCHING

A. Match the following individuals with the appropriate description.

_____1. Cornelius Vanderbilt   a. speculator who built lines just to sell them to competitors

_____2. Thomas Scott   b. shipping magnate who put together his own railroad trunk line

_____3. Charles Crocker   c. financier who dominated American railroading

_____4. Jay Gould   d. construction chief for the Union Pacific

_____5. J. P. Morgan   e. construction chief for the Central Pacific

                                    f. brilliant businessperson who helped organize the largest business enterprise of the 1870s

B. Match the following individuals with their invention or process.

_____1. Cyrus W. Field   a. photographic process that led to film

_____2. George Eastman   b. meat "dissembly" plants

_____3. Gustavus F. Swift   c. telephone

_____4. Alexander Graham Bell   d. electric streetcar system

_____5. George Westinghouse   e. improved transatlantic cable

                                    f. use of high-voltage alternating current

COMPLETION

Answer the question or complete the statement by filling in the blanks with the correct word or words.

1. The exhibit that attracted the most attention at the 1876 Centennial Exposition was the _____.

2. _____ described the locomotives as "Type of the modern-emblem of motion and power. . . ."

3. The _____ first divided the United States into four time zones.

4. Many railroad speculators _____ their stock; that is, they distributed more stock than the value of their company's assets.

5. Financier _____ combined Carnegie's company with others to establish the United States Steel Corporation.

6. To centralize control of Standard Oil, John D. Rockefeller led in the establishment of the first modern _____ in 1882.

7. Between the 1850s and 1890s, the number of patents issued to inventors increased from fewer than _____ a year to _____ a year.

8. In 1867, American businesses spent some _____ million on advertising; in 1900, over _____ million.

9. Sears, Roebuck and Montgomery Ward started as _____ businesses.

10. Between 1880 and 1914, the average American worker's wages rose about _____ per year.

TRUE/FALSE

Mark the following statements either T (True) or F (False).

_____1. By 1900, America's manufacturing output exceeded that of Great Britain, France, and Germany combined.

_____2. Although the railroads tied together the major cities, they left America's villages and rural areas in greater isolation than ever.

_____3. Because of waste and corruption, government grants for railroad construction probably did more harm than good.

_____4. Andrew Carnegie favored workers and unions far more than most industrialists of his era.

_____5. J. P. Morgan and John D. Rockefeller advocated vigorous competition among corporations because it would improve the quality of goods and services and reduce prices.

_____6. Soon after Rockefeller established his oil trust, other highly competitive industries, including whiskey, lead, and sugar, adopted the monopolistic method.

_____7. The establishment of the Menlo Park research laboratory may have been as important as any invention by Thomas Edison.

_____8. White, native-born Protestants benefited most from early industrial society.

_____9. In the late nineteenth century, workers often used court injunctions to protect themselves and their unions from corporate strike-breaking activities.

_____10. To increase their numbers, early unions opened membership to both women and African Americans.

MULTIPLE CHOICE

Circle the one alternative that *best* completes the statement or answers the question.

1. The 1876 Centennial Exposition focused mainly on
   a. American history.
   b. machinery.
   c. popular culture.
   d. art and literature.

2. Which of the following did *not* contribute significantly to American industrialization of the late nineteenth century?
   a. abundant resources
   b. rapid population growth
   c. international free trade
   d. investor confidence

3. Which of the following lists industrial developments in their proper chronological order?
   a. the completion of the first transcontinental railroad, formation of the first trust, formation of U.S. Steel Corporation
   b. the formation of U.S. Steel, formation of the first trust, completion of the first transcontinental railroad
   c. the formation of the first trust, completion of the first transcontinental railroad, formation of U.S. Steel
   d. none of the above

4. Which of the following industries was *not* transformed by a nineteenth-century invention by either Alexander Graham Bell or Thomas Alva Edison?
   a. communications
   b. power
   c. entertainment
   d. textiles

5. Why did trusts form in the late nineteenth century?
   a. to increase efficiency
   b. to reduce costs
   c. to decrease competition
   d. to increase the supply of capital

6. The Bessemer process transformed the steel industry because it
   a. required less capital.
   b. used far less labor.
   c. produced more durable steel.
   d. used cheap ore.

7. John D. Rockefeller's methods for defeating competitors did *not* include
   a. high quality and low prices.
   b. threats and bribery.
   c. spies and harassment.
   d. financial support from J. P. Morgan.

8. According to Herbert Gutman, industrialization transformed the "culture of work." Which of the following best states his meaning?
   a. Industrialization dramatically increased leisure time.
   b. Workers eagerly adopted the new technology because it made their work so much easier.
   c. The new technology often required difficult and demeaning adaptations to premodern work patterns.
   d. Low pay led to frequent worker resistance, especially "sit-down" strikes.

9. Which of these produced *no* innovations for marketing or merchandising?
   a. N. W. Ayer and Son
   b. Finley Peter Dunne
   c. R. H. Macy
   d. Marshall Field

10. It took about $600 a year to have a decent standard of living in the 1890s, while workers earned a yearly average of
    a. $300–$400
    b. $400–$500
    c. $500–600
    d. $600–$700

11. When a substantial number of women entered a profession,
    a. they became a majority of its workers.
    b. men took its management positions.
    c. many men left for jobs in other fields.
    d. all of the above

12. According to social historian Stephan Thernstrom, what was the extent of social mobility in America in the early industrial era?
    a. almost none
    b. some, but not much
    c. substantial, but limited
    d. a great deal

13. Which of the following best describes the early American Federation of Labor?
    a. an alliance of industrial unions that tried to change the economic system
    b. an alliance of industrial unions that tried to improve wages and working conditions
    c. an alliance of craft unions that tried to change the economic system
    d. an alliance of craft unions that tried to improve wages and working conditions

14. Which of the following best describes the Knights of Labor?
    a. a union of "producers" aimed at making "each man his own employer"
    b. a union of "producers aimed only at improving wages and working conditions"
    c. a federation of industrial unions aimed at making "each man his own employer"
    d. a federation of craft unions aimed only at improving wages and working conditions

15. The Haymarket riot weakened the labor movement because it
    a. linked labor and anarchism in the minds of many people.
    b. demonstrated the ineffectiveness of unions.
    c. revealed the violent nature of unions.
    d. initiated the use of court injunctions against strikes.

THOUGHT QUESTIONS

To check your understanding of the key issues of this period, solve the following problems:

1. Was the industrial "revolution" inevitable, or could Americans have maintained a more agricultural economy?

2. Why did so many Americans accept, and even applaud, ruthless methods used to accumulate personal fortunes?

3. Are our early industrialists best described as "captains of industry" or as "robber barons"?

4. What were the costs and the benefits of the development of an American "community of consumers"?

5. Why were so many workers rebellious at a time when real wages were rising?

6. American workers could have gained more by adopting the program of the Knights of Labor rather than that of the American Federation of Labor. True or false? Explain your answer.

CHAPTER 19

TOWARD AN URBAN SOCIETY: 1877–1900

SUMMARY
The development of American cities radically altered the nation's social environment and problems.

THE LURE OF THE CITY
In the late nineteenth century, people flocked to the city, drawn by economic opportunity and the promise of a more exciting life.

Skyscrapers and Suburbs
Between 1870 and 1900, cities grew on the basis of a new technology of metal-frame skyscrapers, electric elevators, streetcar systems, and green suburbs, producing an increasingly stratified and fragmented society.

Tenements and Privies
Immigrants from abroad joined rural Americans in search of jobs in the nation's cities.

Strangers in a New Land
The "new" immigrants turned to their families, churches, schools, and ethnic organizations to endure the economic and social stresses of industrial capitalism.

The House That Tweed Built
Political "machines" provided some needed services for these immigrants while enriching themselves by exploiting the dependency of the cities' new residents.

LIFE IN AMERICA, 1877
The development of an urban society transformed America.

Manners and Mores
Victorian morality, manners and mores declined in the face of rapid changes.

Leisure and Entertainment
Technology brought a variety of new forms of leisure and entertainment.

Family Life
Economic changes also produced new roles for women and the family. Working-class families no longer toiled together but did maintain the strong ties needed to survive the urban industrial struggle; middle-class families became more isolated; homemakers attempted to construct a sphere of domesticity as a haven from rampaging materialism.

Changing Views: A Growing Assertiveness Among Women
Americans also began to change their views about women, demonstrating a limited but growing acceptance of working women, divorce, sexuality, and women's rights and related causes.

Educating the Masses
With the development of childhood as a distinct time of life, Americans placed greater emphasis on education with a structured curriculum and a longer school day. The South lagged behind in such educational changes.

Higher Education
Colleges expanded in size, broadened their curriculum, developed the first American graduate schools, and provided more educational opportunities for women, but still provided little opportunity for African Americans and other minorities.

THE STIRRINGS OF REFORM
In spite of the period's "social Darwinism," increasing numbers of Americans proposed the need for reforms.

Progress and Poverty
Henry George launched critical studies of the new urban America with his book *Progress and Poverty*.

New Currents in Social Thought
Social thinkers challenged the tenets of social Darwinism with a new emphasis on the influence of environmental deprivation on poverty.

The Settlement Houses
New professional social workers, many of them women, established settlement houses to improve slum conditions by providing education, training and other social services, and by working to abolish child labor.

A Crisis in Social Welfare
In responding to the depression of 1893, social workers, many of them women, introduced new methods such as settlement houses that approached poverty as a social problem rather than an individual shortcoming.

LEARNING OBJECTIVES

After mastering this chapter, you should be able to

1. Trace the journeys of the new immigrants from their places of origin to America, and explain their adaptation to urban stresses and their effect on American cities.

2. Specify the role of skyscrapers, suburbs and tenements in the rise of the city.

3. Identify and describe the major problems of American central cities in the Victorian era.

4. Explain and evaluate the operation of the early political "machines."

5. Describe the most common form of food, housing and medical care in 1877.

6. Identify and describe the principal moral values and issues of Victorian America.

7. Describe the most popular forms of pastimes and entertainments in Victorian America.

8. Delineate the changing roles of both women and the family in America from 1877–1900.

9. Describe the changes taking place in public education between 1877–1900.

10. Describe the major changes taking place in American higher education, 1877–1900.

11. Compare and contrast the educational and civil rights policies of Booker T. Washington and W. E. B. Du Bois.

12. Describe the principal tenets of social Darwinism and the opposing reform theory, including some of the specific arguments of major proponents of each view.

13. Trace the rise of professional social workers in the settlement houses and in the depression of 1893.

GLOSSARY

To build your social science vocabulary, familiarize yourself with the following terms:

1. **pilanthropy** charitable donation or action. "Private philanthropy . . . spurred growth in higher education."

2. **land-grant institutions** colleges and universities established with large tracts of land granted to states by the federal government under the Morrill Land Grant Act of 1862. "The act fostered 69 'land-grant' institutions."

3. **nuclear family** the immediate family of father, mother, and children. ". . . most immigrant families were nuclear in structure. . . ."

4. **nativists** those who support the interests of the native born as opposed to those of immigrants. ". . . a fact that worried nativists opposed to immigration."

5. **wards** administrative and political districts of a city. ". . . one of whose wards had a population density of 334,000 people per square mile."

6. **"boss"** one who controls a political organization. ". . . they were headed by a strong, influential leader—the boss'. . . ."

7. **precinct captain** a political leader of the ward, precinct, or neighborhood level, subordinate to the "boss." ". . . a network of ward and precinct captains, each of whom looked after his local constituents."

8. **mores** customs of a group or society that are considered so important that they usually have legal sanction. "Mores changed. . . ."

9. **mortality** the death rate, usually expressed as a ratio of the number of deaths to the total population. "Infant mortality declined. . . ."

10. **behavioral** a school of social or psychological studies founded on facts of human behavior. "William James . . . laid the foundations of modern behavioral psychology. . . ."

11. **census** an official counting of the population and its constituent groups. "In 1882, the United States Census Bureau took the first census of working women. . . ."

12. **common law** law based on court decision and custom, as opposed to written, statutory law. "One important change occurred in . . . common law doctrine. . . ."

13. **chattel** movable, personal property. "Under that doctrine, wives were chattel of their husbands. . . ."

14. **Victorian** pertaining to the reign of England's Queen Victoria (1837–1901) or to its stuffy, prudish morality. "a bestseller that . . . challenged Victorian notions. . . ."

15. **dogmatism** insistent support for principles treated as truths. "Ely . . . attacked classical economics for its dogmatism. . . ."

IDENTIFICATION

Briefly identify the meaning and significance of the following terms.

1. the "new woman" _____

_____

2. Booker T. Washington _____

_____

3. "new" immigrants _____

_____

4. tenements_____

_____

5. political "machines"_____

_____

6. social Darwinism _____

_____

7. Henry George _____

_____

8. Social Gospel_____

_____

9. settlement houses_____

_____

10. social workers _____

_____

MATCHING

A. Match the following authors with the appropriate titles and themes.

_____ 1. William Graham Sumner   **a.** *Applied Christianity*; attacks competition and urges cooperation between employees and employers

_____ 2. Thorstein Veblen   **b.** *What Social Classes Owe to Each Other*; holds that government aid to the poor interferes with evolution

_____ 3. Edward Bellamy   **c.** *Looking Backward, 2000–1887*; describes a socialist utopia of the future

_____ 4. Washington Gladden   **d.** *Progress and Poverty*; urges a tax on land to equalize wealth

_____ 5. Lillian Wald   **e.** *The Theory of the Leisure Class*; says business elites display "conspicuous consumption"

                                                        f. *The House on Henry Street*; describes a New York settlement house

B. Match the following reformers with the appropriate description.

_____ 1. Stanton Coit   **a.** devoted life's work to solving the problem of child labor

_____ 2. Jane Addams   **b.** founded Hull House in Chicago's slums

_____ 3. Florence Kelley   **c.** worked as unskilled laborer, then described findings in *The Workers* (1897)

_____ 4. Walter Wyckoff   **d.** borrowed the settlement house idea from England

_____ 5. Robert Woods   **e.** described tenements in *How the Other Half Lives*

                                                        f. focused on Boston school dropouts

COMPLETION

Answer the question or complete the statement by filling in the blanks with the correct word or words.

1. A former shoe salesman named _____ conducted mass revivals across the country.

2. Educated upper-class individuals who worked to end political corruption—including Thomas Nast, George William Curtis, and E. L. Godkin—were called _____.

3. In 1873, Congress prohibited the transporting or mailing of "obscene, lewd, or lascivious" articles with the _____ Law.

4. Courtship often occurred at an outdoor game called _____.

5. Critics of the turn of the century denounced as "vulgar, filthy, and suggestive" a new form of music called _____.

6. One of the period's most widely used textbooks, written by a language professor, was called _____.

7. By 1890, the number of Americans who were foreign-born had reached _____, _____ percent of the total population.

8. The leader of a group of Chicago architects who led in the innovation of new forms of building was _____.

9. The member of Tammany Hall who provided a model of the political "machine" was _____.

TRUE/FALSE

Mark the following statements either T (True) or F (False).

_____1. By 1877, technological change had produced a set of sharply defined political issues.

_____2. Because of their rather sedate taste in entertainment, nineteenth-century Americans opposed such frivolities as circuses and melodramas.

_____3. Between 1877 and 1890, the American family was declining in its economic function but increasing in emotional significance.

_____ 4. In the late nineteenth century, American colleges and universities moved away from the traditional classical curriculum toward "reality and practicality."

_____ 5. In the years 1877 to 1890, African Americans enjoyed more educational opportunities than did women.

_____ 6. Charles Guiteau's trial for the assassination of President Garfield turned on conflicting theories of mental illness.

_____ 7. The American Protective Association developed primarily as a neighborhood anticrime, vigilante group.

_____ 8. In the 1880s American cities suffered less crowding, pollution, and crime than do today's cities.

_____ 9. Clarence Darrow argued that the "unjust condition of human life" produced criminals.

_____ 10. The new social workers of the late nineteenth century produced theoretical and utopian studies that neglected specifics and details.

MULTIPLE CHOICE

Circle the one alternative that *best* completes the statement or answers the question.

1. By 1900, most Americans lived
   a. in central cities.
   b. in the suburbs.
   c. in the central cities or suburbs.
   d. in the small towns or on farms.

2. What was the average life expectancy of Americans in 1900?
   a. thirty-seven years, but only thirty-five years for African Americans
   b. forty-seven years, but only forty-five years for African Americans
   c. forty-seven years, but only thirty-three years for African Americans
   d. fifty-seven years, but only fifty-three years for African Americans

3. Late nineteenth-century reforms benefiting women included
   a. increased status for housewives.
   b. laws granting women control of their earnings.
   c. the right to vote.
   d. laws granting women equal pay for equal work.

4. Educational changes in the years 1877 to 1900 did *not* include
   a. a decrease in illiteracy.
   b. education as a field of university study.
   c. development of the kindergarten.
   d. compulsory school attendance in all states.

5. In response to Booker T. Washington's policies of political passivity and vocational training, W. E. B. Du Bois proposed
   a. political activism and intellectual education.
   b. political passivity and intellectual education.
   c. political activism and vocational training.
   d. political passivity and vocational training.

6. Which of the following places events in the correct chronological order?
   a. Morrill Land Grant Act, *Plessy v. Ferguson*, establishment of Tuskegee Institute
   b. *Plessy v. Ferguson*, Morrill Land Grant Act, establishment of Tuskegee Institute
   c. establishment of Tuskegee Institute, Morrill Land Grant Act, *Plessy v. Ferguson*
   d. Morrill Land Grant Act, establishment of Tuskegee Institute, *Plessy v. Ferguson*

7. During the late nineteenth century, American women did not
   a. move into the work force in greater numbers.
   b. cease to be chattel of their husbands in the law of many states.
   c. espouse fewer reforms than earlier generations of American women.
   d. all of the above

8. As a solution to the poverty in modern society, Henry George proposed
   a. to let nature take its evolutionary course.
   b. to replace all taxes with a "single tax" on land.
   c. to establish a socialist utopia in which the government owns the means of production.
   d. to establish worker and farmer "cooperatives" to own the means of production.

9. Herbert Spencer's social Darwinism held that
   a. humans advanced civilization with social cooperation.
   b. society should help the rich and powerful to encourage "survival of the fittest."
   c. government should help the poor to overcome the "struggle to survive."
   d. society evolved by adapting to the environment through social selection.

10. Leaders of the "settlement house" movement tried to
    a. help immigrants to learn American history and language while preserving their own ethnic heritage.
    b. reduce school dropouts and regulate child labor.
    c. create for the city small-town values and community.
    d. all of the above

11. Which of the following authors argued that the American ideal of women's "innocence" really meant their ignorance?
    a. Charlotte Perkins Gilman in *Women and Economics*
    b. Edward Bliss Foote in *Plain Home Talk of Love, Marriage, and Parentage*
    c. Bessie and Marie Von Vorst in *The Woman Who Toils*
    d. Helen Campbell in *Women Wage Earners*

12. Changes in higher education included all of the following *except*
    a. an increased number of colleges and universities.
    b. the first separate graduate schools.
    c. an increased emphasis on a classical curriculum.
    d. more educational opportunities for women.

13. According to George Washington Plunkett, political "machines" survived because they
    a. offered good, honest government.
    b. offered needed services for the poor.
    c. bought votes with "honest graft."
    d. all of the above

14. Significant medical developments in Victorian America included all of the following *except*
    a. prevention of tuberculosis, typhoid, and diphtheria.
    b. discovery that germs cause infection and disease.
    c. relatively safe and painless surgery.
    d. more antiseptic practices in childbirth.

15. Which approach to poverty was used by professional social workers but not by church and charity volunteers?
    a. reform of individual families
    b. alleviation of underlying conditions of poverty
    c. help in alleviating the suffering caused by economic depression

THOUGHT QUESTIONS

To check your understanding of the key issues of this period, solve the following problems:

1. Many historians have emphasized the role of the western frontier in shaping American society. Should we place greater emphasis on the significance of the city? Why or why not?

2. What factors led to the rapid development of the city in the late nineteenth century?

3. Why have urban Americans been more tolerant of individual social and cultural differences?

4. How did the reform approach of urban Americans differ from that of agrarian populists?

5. Social workers tried to alleviate the conditions of poverty that political machines exploited. To what extent have they succeeded? Have they simply transformed the dependency of the urban poor?

6. On the whole, has our society gained more than it lost in the transition from rural to urban?

7. In what ways did ethnic pluralism shape the American city? American society?

CHAPTER 20

POLITICAL REALIGNMENTS IN THE 1890S

SUMMARY
Economic depression dominated the 1890s and reshaped political alignments and attitudes.

POLITICS OF STALEMATE
America's white male voters of the 1870s and 1880s displayed keen interest in partisan politics. Southern states increasingly disfranchised black men.

The Party Deadlock
Democrats emphasized decentralized power, Republicans a more active national government; but the closeness of electoral politics and disillusionment with Civil War centralization stalemated national government.

Experiments in the States
Most governmental action, and especially the new regulatory commissions and bureaus, occurred at the state and local level.

Reestablishing Presidential Power
Between 1880 and 1900, American presidents succeeded in reasserting the authority of their office, which had been weakened considerably by the Johnson impeachment, the Grant scandals, and the electoral controversy of 1876. By the late 1890s, they had laid the basis for the modern powerful presidency.

REPUBLICANS IN POWER: THE BILLION-DOLLAR CONGRESS
In 1888, the Republicans broke the electoral stalemate by winning control of the presidency and both houses of Congress.

Tariffs, Trusts, and Silver
In the following two years, the Republicans enacted a significant legislative program of the McKinley Tariff Act, the Sherman Antitrust Act and the Sherman Silver Purchase Act.

The 1890 Elections
Americans rejected that activism by crushing the Republicans in the elections of 1890.

THE RISE OF THE POPULIST MOVEMENT
By the summer of 1890, Farmers' Alliance organizers were recruiting huge numbers of unhappy farmers.

The Farm Problem
Populism surged as a response to an agrarian sense of social and economic loss that was not altogether realistic.

The Fast-Growing Farmers' Alliance
Farmers organized the Grange and the Farmers' Alliance in pursuit of the reforms of the Ocala Demands. In the South, the Alliance enjoyed considerable success within the Democratic party; in the North and West, it successfully ran many of its own candidates.

The People's Party
In 1892, the Alliance led the formation of the Populist party, which collected over one million votes for its 1892 presidential candidate, but the party then began to lose strength.

THE CRISIS OF THE DEPRESSION
Grover Cleveland and the Democratic party swept the election of 1892 but then faced a severe depression following the Panic of 1893.

Coxey's Army and the Pullman Strike
The depression led to protests demanding relief for workers and farmers, including a march on Washington by Coxey's army and the Pullman strike, which shut down the railroads of the West and produced the Socialist leader Eugene Debs. President Cleveland defeated the strike with a violent confrontation between federal troops and a mob made up mostly of nonstrikers.

The Miners of the Midwest
The depression also led to a strike of bituminous coal mines by the new United Mine Workers. The violence which followed pitted workers against capital but also divided the "old" mostly English and Irish miners and the "new" miners from southern and eastern Europe.

A Beleaguered President
President Cleveland blamed the depression on the Sherman Silver Purchase Act and led its repeal in 1893, which split and, in combination with the depression, wrecked the Democratic party.

Depression Politics
The depression led to a new Republican supremacy and made the Democratic party little more than a southern, sectional party.

CHANGING ATTITUDES
The depression also changed the country's traditional social views. Many Americans now saw poverty as a failure of the economy rather than the individual, so they demanded reforms to help the poor and unemployed, an important step toward national authority and activism.

Everybody Works but Father
More women and children worked at jobs made available to them because they were paid less than men.

Changing Themes in Literature
Realistic and naturalistic writers portrayed everyday life in a new, sometimes deterministic manner, including, for example, Mark Twain, William Dean Howells, Stephen Crane, Frank Norris, and Theodore Dreiser.

THE PRESIDENTIAL ELECTION OF 1896
The Republican dominance initiated in 1894 continued with the victory of the Republican McKinley over the Democrat Bryan.

The Mystique of Silver
Silver became a central, symbolic issue. Many believed its free coinage could end the depression; it also came to represent the interests of the common people.

The Republicans and Gold
McKinley and the Republicans promised a return to the gold standard, which they claimed would end the depression.

The Democrats and Silver
Although split over silver, the Democrats endorsed free silver and nominated William Jennings Bryan after he captured the convention with the oratory of his "Cross of Gold" speech. McKinley won the election handily.

THE MCKINLEY ADMINISTRATION
The new government enjoyed prosperity, raised the tariff, demonetized silver, and prodded its party to shift from promoting to regulating industrialism. By the time of McKinley's assassination and Theodore Roosevelt's ascent to the presidency, the Republican party had clearly emerged as the dominant party, as Americans rallied to reform the system that had produced the depression of the 1890s.

LEARNING OBJECTIVES

After mastering this chapter, you should be able to

1. Discuss the stalemate of partisan politics in the 1870s and 1880s.

2. Explain the rise of the early state regulatory commissions.

3. Trace the reassertion of presidential power from 1876 to 1888.

4. Identify and describe the legislation passed by the Republican party in 1890 and the voters' response to that "billion-dollar Congress."

5. Describe and evaluate the American agrarians' grievances in the late nineteenth century.

6. Trace the growth of the farmers' protest from the Grange through the Farmers' Alliance.

7. Detail the establishment of the Populist party, its platform, and its first presidential election.

8. Discuss the march of "Coxey's Army" and the "great" Pullman strike of 1894.

9. Explain the divisions between capital and labor and between "old" and "new" miners in the Midwestern coal strike of 1894.

10. Describe the changes in American attitudes toward poverty brought by the depression of the 1890s.

11. Describe the changes in the American work force brought by the depression of the 1890s.

12. Trace the rise of the new realist and naturalist movements in American literature.

13. Explain how the silver issue served as a symbol for a social and political movement.

14. Compare and contrast the Democratic and Republican presidential campaigns of 1896.

15. Evaluate the role of the election and administration of William McKinley in the emergence of modern urban, industrial government and politics.

GLOSSARY

To build your social science vocabulary, familiarize yourself with the following terms:

1. **poll tax** a tax charged against each person, often for the right to vote. "In 1877, Georgia adopted the poll tax. . . ."

2. **literacy test** a test of reading ability used to prevent African Americans and others from registering to vote. ". . . the famous 'grandfather clause,' which used a literacy test. . . ."

3. **commissions** groups charged with a public function, especially regulation. "... state bureaus and commissions were established to regulate the new industrial society."

4. **bipartisan** supported by or consisting of members of two political parties. "... the act created a bipartisan Civil Service Commission...."

5. **public domain** without legal protection of patent, copyright, or registration; government-owned land. "He ... forced ... companies to surrender millions of acres of fraudulently occupied public domain...."

6. **reciprocity** a policy whereby countries grant corresponding, mutual rights or privileges to the citizens of each, especially in trade relations. "... it also included a novel reciprocity provision that allowed the president to lower duties if other countries did the same."

7. **trust** a combination of businesses to eliminate competition and control prices. "It declared illegal "... 'every ... combination in the form of trust ... in restraint of trade....' "

8. **lien** a claim against property as security for satisfaction of an obligation. "... many southern farmers were trapped in the crop lien system that kept them in debt."

9. **cooperative** jointly owned and operated for mutual benefit. "... between 1886 and 1892, cooperative enterprises blossomed in the South."

10. **platform** a statement of the public principles and policies of a political party or group. "... the Alliance adopted the Ocala Demands, the platform it pushed for as long as it existed."

11. **special session** an unscheduled legislative session called by an executive for specific purposes. "... Cleveland summoned Congress into special session...."

12. **romanticism** a style of art and literature emphasizing emotion, imagination and freedom of form. "In the years after the Civil War, literature often reflected the mood of romanticism...."

13. **realism** a style of art and literature emphasizing realistic depiction of everyday life. "... a number of talented authors began to reject ... escapism, turning instead to realism...."

14. **naturalism** a style of art and literature emphasizing a detailed, clinical, deterministic view of life. "The depression also gave point to a growing movement in literature toward ... naturalism."

15. **imperialism** the policy of achieving economic or political power over other nations. "Bryan stressed the issues of imperialism and the trusts...."

IDENTIFICATION

Briefly identify the meaning and significance of the following terms.

1. state commissions _____
   _____

2. Populism _____
   _____

3. Coxey's army _____
   _____

4. Pullman strike _____
   _____

5. Grover Cleveland _____
   _____

6. realism _____
   _____

7. naturalism _____
   _____

8. free silver coinage _____
   _____

9. William Jennings Bryan _____
   _____

10. William McKinley _____
    _____

MATCHING

A. Match the following court decisions with the appropriate description.

____1. *Minor v. Happersett*

____2. *Munn v. Illinois*

____3. *Wabash R. R. v. Illinois*

____4. *United States v. E. C. Knight*

____5. *In re Debs*

a. declared that a state could regulate private property" affected with the public interest"

b. endorsed the use of an injunction in a labor strike

c. upheld the use of literacy tests for voter registration

d. upheld a state's power to deny women the right to vote

e. ruled that a state could not regulate commerce that extended beyond its borders

f. ruled that the Sherman Antitrust Act did not apply to manufacturing

B. Match the following authors with the appropriate description.

____1. Mark Twain

____2. William Dean Howells

____3. Stephen Crane

____4. Frank Norris

____5. Theodore Dreiser

a. attacked the power of the big corporations in *The Octopus*

b. portrayed a grim world of the exhausted factory worker in *Sister Carrie*

c. changed American prose style by replacing literary language with common speech and dialect

d. portrayed wise youth explaining currency to famous people

e. described the evils of industrial society in a utopian novel, *A Traveler from Altruria*

f. depicted the impact of poverty in *Maggie: A Girl of the Streets*

COMPLETION

Answer the question or complete the statement by filling in the blanks with the correct word or words.

1. The Speaker of the House who broke a legislative deadlock with significant changes in congressional rules was _____.

2. In 1883, Congress legislated the establishment of a Civil Service Commission with the _____ Act.

3. Foremost in the Ocala Demands of the Farmers' Alliance was the _____.

4. Republican leaders Roscoe Conkling and President James Garfield divided over the issue of _____.

5. In the presidential elections of 1876 through 1896, an average percentage of about _____ of the electorate voted.

6. In 1887, Congress provided for federal investigation and oversight of railroads with the establishment of the _____.

7. In 1892, the Populist party nominated _____ for the presidency.

8. The Republican leader who managed William McKinley's 1896 presidential campaign was _____.

9. William Harvey extolled the merits of silver coinage in a book entitled _____.

10. In 1897, Republicans raised the tariff rates to record levels with the _____ Tariff.

TRUE/FALSE

Mark the following statements either T (True) or F (False).

_____1. In 1892, southern Populists tried to unite black and white farmers.

_____2. In the 1870s and 1880s, the Democratic party supported measures by the federal government to promote the national economy.

_____3. While the Republican party of the 1870s and 1880s supported increased power and activity at the national level of government, the Democrats emphasized decentralized government with more power and activity at the state and local level.

_____ 4. In the election of 1894, Democrats won the greatest victory in congressional history.

_____ 5. During the depression of the 1890s, an increasing number of Americans blamed unemployment on individual failure.

_____ 6. Between the years 1877 and 1888, the American presidency lost power as Congress reasserted much power and authority that it had lost during the period of the Civil War and Reconstruction.

_____ 7. Southern Democrats Thomas Watson and Leonidas Polk used fraud and manipulation to defeat Populist candidates in 1892.

_____ 8. Between 1877 and 1900, southern states disfranchised African Americans with laws establishing poll taxes, "eight box" balloting, literacy tests, and "grandfather" clauses.

_____ 9. In 1893, economic overexpansion led to a panic and depression which President Cleveland mistakenly blamed on the Sherman Silver Purchase Act.

_____ 10. The central belief of silverites was a quantity theory of money.

MULTIPLE CHOICE

Circle the one alternative that *best* completes the statement or answers the question.

1. The McKinley Tariff did not
   a. raise the tariff rate by 4 percent to the highest level it had ever been.
   b. use duties to promote new industries like the tinplate used for the new canned foods.
   c. give the president power to reciprocate if other countries lowered tariff rates.
   d. permit the president to raise rates to protect threatened American industries.

2. The Colored Farmers' National Alliance ended when
   a. a posse lynched fifteen strikers.
   b. prices on cotton increased significantly.
   c. southern planters used strike breakers in the cotton fields.
   d. the Farmers' Alliance leadership expelled all African Americans from the organization.

3. In 1890, the American electorate
   a. rejected Democratic legislative activism by crushing the party in the congressional elections.
   b. rejected Republican legislative activism by crushing the party in the congressional elections.
   c. rejected the legislative passiveness of both major parties by electing many third-party and especially Populist candidates to Congress.
   d. rejected Republican passiveness by crushing the party in the congressional elections.

4. In the elections of 1890 the Democrats
   a. crushed the Republicans.
   b. were crushed by the Republicans.
   c. narrowly defeated the Republicans.
   d. were narrowly defeated by the Republicans.

5. Which of the following is *not* true of American farmers in the 1865–1890 period?
   a. Prices for their crops declined.
   b. Their purchasing power declined.
   c. Farm mortgages were common.
   d. Their productivity increased.

6. Which best describes the source of agrarian anger and protest in the late nineteenth century?
   a. Farm prices fell far more than did prices for other commodities.
   b. Railroad rates increased dramatically between 1870 and 1900.
   c. Farmers perceived their social and economic position as declining throughout the period.
   d. all of the above

7. In 1894, Jacob S. Coxey led a march on Washington to demand
   a. road construction financed with paper money.
   b. coinage of silver at a ratio to gold of 16 to 1.
   c. an immediate and significant reduction of the tariff.
   d. a "subtreasury" system for American farmers.

8. Leaders of the Southern Farmers' Alliance
   a. formed the first major People's party.
   b. tried to capture the Democratic party.
   c. eschewed politics for more radical methods.
   d. often crossed over to the Republican party.

9. In the Pullman Strike of 1894, Cleveland's intervention
   a. gave business the court injunction as a new weapon against labor.
   b. ensured the success of the strike.
   c. failed to end the strike.
   d. gave workers the protection of a court injunction.

10. Which group was the first to be seriously affected by the wave of "new" immigrants to America from southern and eastern Europe?
    a. railroad workers
    b. midwestern farmers
    c. midwestern miners
    d. southern sharecroppers

11. Which of the following lists events in the correct chronological order?
    a. Republican policy to regulate industry, Panic of 1893, Republican policy to promote industry
    b. Republican policy to promote industry, Republican policy to regulate industry, Panic of 1893
    c. Republican policy to promote industry, Panic of 1893, Republican policy to regulate industry
    d. none of the above

12. Support for free silver coinage grew rapidly from 1894 to 1896 because
    a. the issue offered a simple, compelling answer for economic crisis.
    b. workers joined farmers in support of coinage.
    c. Cleveland Democrats joined workers in support of coinage.
    d. all of the above

13. Which best describes the decision that shattered the Populist party in 1896?
    a. the endorsement for the presidency of the Democratic candidate William Jennings Bryan
    b. the admission of African Americans to the party's ranks
    c. the nomination of their own candidate, James Weaver, for the presidency
    d. the expulsion of all African American members in an attempt to attract more southern support

14. McKinley's first term in office was characterized by
    a. increased economic prosperity.
    b. gold discoveries that inflated the currency.
    c. presidential activism.
    d. all of the above

15. By 1900 McKinley had begun prodding the Republican party toward a new policy of
    a. monetary inflation through silver coinage.
    b. promoting economic growth with subsidies and tariffs.
    c. regulating and controlling industry.
    d. another increase in tariff rates.

THOUGHT QUESTIONS

To check your understanding of the key issues of this period, solve the following problems:

1. Why were the presidential elections of the "Gilded Age" so very close?

2. The Populists' political rebellion defined the American response to industrialism. True or false? Explain your answer.

3. What was the basic difference in the approaches of the Republican and Democratic parties to the problems of the 1890s? Why did Americans choose the Republican approach?

4. Was the silver issue a symbol of class differences? of sectional differences? Explain your answers.

5. What determined the outcome of the Populist-Democratic contest in the South? Did class differences play a significant role? Did race play a significant role?

CHAPTER 21

TOWARD EMPIRE

AMERICA LOOKS OUTWARD
In contrast to prior expansion into contiguous territories intended for settlement and annexation, the United States in the 1890s acquired island colonies intended as naval bases and commercial outposts for the expansion and protection of American markets.

Catching the Spirit of Empire
Stimulated by a closing frontier and an expanding economy at home, the United States became increasingly interested in the worldwide scramble for colonies in the latter part of the nineteenth century. Advocates of Anglo-Saxon racial superiority exhorted expansion of American trade and dominion as both our duty and destiny in "civilizing" the less advanced regions of the world.

Foreign Policy Approaches, 1867–1900
During this era, American policymakers sought to avoid entanglements in Europe while expanding American trade, and perhaps territory, in Latin American and Asia. The United States reasserted the Monroe Doctrine and promoted Pan-American interests.

The Lure of Hawaii and Samoa
The Hawaiian and Samoan Islands attracted Americans primarily as stepping stones to the valuable trade of the Far East. American residents in Hawaii instigated a revolution and the creation of a republican government in 1893, but the United States resisted annexation of the islands until 1898. After first acquiring a naval station in Samoa in 1878, the United States divided the island chain with Germany in 1899.

The New Navy
Captain Alfred Thayer Mahan, naval strategist and historian, convinced many Americans of the need for an expanded navy to guarantee the nation's wealth and power. Benjamin F. Tracy, secretary of the navy under President Benjamin Harrison, pushed Congress to begin a build-up program that would move the United States from twelfth among world navies in 1889 to third in 1900.

A WAR FOR PRINCIPLE
In 1895, economic depression and discontent with Spanish rule led to revolution in Cuba. Spain responded with a policy of brutal repression. Exaggerated accounts of Spanish atrocities by America's "yellow press"; the publication of a letter insulting President McKinley from the Spanish ambassador in Washington; and the sinking of the American battleship *Maine* in Havana harbor all contributed to a growing clamor for United States intervention in the war on behalf of

Cuban independence. Dissatisfied with Spain's response to Cuban and American demands, President McKinley called for war in April 1898.

"A Splendid Little War"
Congress and the American public responded enthusiastically to war. More soldiers volunteered to fight than could be trained, fed, or equipped. The war lasted only ten weeks and resulted in relatively few American deaths, more to tropical diseases than battle, prompting the soon-to-be Secretary of State John Hay's famous observation of the conflict as "a splendid little war."

"Smoked Yankees"
Certain that African American men could resist tropical diseases, United States military officials recruited them as soldiers. Although subjected to segregation and discrimination, these "smoked Yankees" (as the Spanish troops referred to them) responded bravely and played a crucial role in the American invasion and takeover of Cuba.

The Course of the War
American military operations began with a stunning naval victory directed by Commodore George Dewey over the Spanish fleet in Manila Bay, resulting in the United States occupation of the Philippine Islands. In the Caribbean, the United States invaded Cuba, captured Santiago, occupied Puerto Rico, and destroyed Spain's only remaining battle fleet, forcing Spain's surrender in August 1898.

DEBATE OVER EMPIRE
The treaty ending the Spanish-American War called for Spanish recognition of Cuban independence; Spanish cession of Puerto Rico, Guam, and the Philippine Islands to the United States; and U.S. payment of $20 million to Spain. Promptly submitted to the Senate for ratification, the treaty set off a storm of debate throughout the country. Members of an Anti-Imperialist League argued that American acquisition of colonies would prove to be undemocratic, costly, and potentially harmful to the interests of labor and racial harmony. Proponents of imperialism repeated the economic, strategic, and intellectual arguments justifying American expansionism. The Senate ratified the treaty in February 1899, with only two votes to spare.

Guerrilla Warfare in the Philippines
Demanding independence, Filipino insurgents led by Emilio Aguinaldo fought a guerrilla war against American takeover of the islands. Proving much more difficult and costly than the war against Spain, the Philippine-American War (1899–1902) convinced American leaders of the need to prepare the island archipelago for eventual self-government.

Governing the Empire
In a series of cases from 1901 to 1904, the Supreme Court ruled that the Constitution does not "follow the flag" and that Congress could extend American constitutional provisions to territories as its saw fit. Cuba was granted "independence," but forced to include the Platt Amendment in her constitution, allowing for special United States privileges, including the right of intervention.

The Open Door
By the end of the nineteenth century, outside powers had carved China into spheres of influence, threatening to reduce or even eliminate American economic interests there. Through a series of diplomatic notes in 1899–1900 urging an "Open Door" in China, Secretary of State John Hay boldly proclaimed a policy that preserved for China some semblance of national authority over its territory and trade and, thus, commercial opportunities equal to other foreign powers for the United States. From 1867 to 1900, the United States had transformed itself from a relatively isolationist nation to one of world power.

LEARNING OBJECTIVES

After mastering this chapter, you should be able to

1. Analyze how and why United States territorial expansion in the 1890s differed from the nation's earlier expansionist moves.

2. explain the economic, strategic, and intellectual factors sparking American interest in overseas expansion in the latter part of the nineteenth century.

3. Illustrate how the United States reasserted the Monroe Doctrine and promoted Pan-American interests during this era.

4. List the territories acquired by the United States during this era and explain the various processes of acquisition.

5. Describe the causes, major events, and consequences of the Spanish-American War.

6. List and explain the factors contributing to the growth of American newspapers in the 1890s, noting especially the popularity of "yellow journalism."

7. evaluate the performance of President McKinley in resolving international problems.

8. Discuss the treatment and performance of African American soldiers during the Spanish-American War.

9. contrast the arguments offered for and against ratification of the treaty ending the Spanish-American War and providing for American colonies.

10. Describe the causes, course, and consequences of the Philippine-American War (1899–1902).

11. Describe the processes by which civil government was established in American territories.

12. Explain the origin and purpose of the Open Door policy in China.

GLOSSARY

To build your social science vocabulary, familiarize yourself with the following terms:

1. **contiguous** touching; adjoining. "Most of these lands were contiguous with existing territories. . . ."

2. **aberration** departure from a moral standard or a normal state. "Historian Samuel F. Bemis described the overseas expansion of the 1890s as 'the great aberration. . . .' ".

3. **impregnable** incapable of being taken; unconquerable. ". . . they could enunciate bold policies . . . while remaining virtually impregnable to foreign attack."

4. **imperialistic** marked by a policy of extending control of one nation or another. "The idea of imperialistic expansion was in the air. . . ."

5. **Pan-American** involving all of the American nations in unified activities. ". . . they based policy on . . . Pan-American unity against the nations of the Old World.."

6. **protectorate** relationship of superior authority assumed by one nation over another; the dependent nation in such a relationship. ". . . its political clauses effectively made Hawaii an American protectorate. . . .".

7. **insular** relating to an island; isolated; detached. "The war with Spain . . . altered older, more insular patterns of thought. . . . "

8. **junta** a committee for political purposes, especially the planning or controlling of a revolutionary action. "Cuban insurgents established a junta in New York City. . . ."

9. **yellow journalism** a technique of newspapers or journals featuring sensationalism as a way to stir attention and increase sales. "But 'yellow' journalism did not cause the war."

10. **autonomy** the quality or state of self-government. "The new government . . . agreed to offer the Cubans some form of autonomy."

11. **deference** respectful regard for another's wishes, opinions, or position. " . . . there was an easygoing familiarity, tempered by the deference that went with hometown wealth. . . . ".

12. **archipelago** a group of islands. "'. . . the president can see but one plain path of duty-the acceptance of the archipelago. . . .' "

13. **assimilation** absorption into the cultural tradition of a population or group. ". . . anti-imperialists argued against assimilation of different races. . . ."

14. **guerrilla tactics**   irregular warfare by independent bands; especially harassment and sabotage. "Aguinaldo and his advisers shifted to guerrilla tactics. . . ."

15. **spheres of influence**   territorial areas in which the political influence or interests of one nation are paramount. ". . . Japan, England, France, Germany, and Russia eyed it covetously, dividing the country into 'spheres of influence. . . .' "

IDENTIFICATION

Briefly identify the meaning and significance of the following terms.

1. Theodore Roosevelt _____

2. James G. Blaine _____

3. Queen Liliuokalani _____

4. William McKinley _____

5. Alfred Thayer Mahan _____

6. The *Maine* _____

7. Anti-Imperialist League _____

8. Emilio Aguinaldo _____

9. William Howard Taft _____

_____

10. Open Door policy _____

_____

MATCHING

A. Match the following nations with the appropriate description.

_____1. Philippine Islands   a. agreed to arbitration of the Alabama claims in the Treaty of Washington in 1871

_____2. China   b. concluded a treaty with Secretary of State William

_____3. Russia   c. erupted in guerrilla warfare following American refusal to recognize its independence

_____4. Venezuela   d. forced to accept a constitutional provision allowing future United States intervention

_____5. Britain   e. accepted United States arbitration, although rarely consulted, in border dispute with British Guiana

          f. subjected to international forces intent upon quelling an internal rebellion

B. Match the following policy statements with the appropriate description.

_____1. Monroe Doctrine   a. established civil government in Puerto Rico, organizing the island as a U.S. territory in 1900

_____2. Teller Amendment   b. denied European nations the right to meddle in the affairs of the Western Hemisphere

_____3. Platt Amendment   c. preserved for China some semblance of national authority in matters of trade

_____4. Open Door   d. provided for the organization of civil government in the Philippines

_____ 5. Foraker Act

    e. empowered the United States to intervene in Cuba to maintain orderly government

    f. pledged that the United States had no intention of annexing Cuba

COMPLETION

Answer the question or complete the statement by filling in the blanks with the correct word or words.

1. In 1898, Theodore Roosevelt recruited an intriguing mixture of college athletes and western frontiersmen for his volunteer cavalry unit known as the _____.

2. The biological theories of _____, when applied by various writers to human and social development, seemed to call for the triumph of the fit and the elimination of the unfit.

3. Congregational minister and fervent expansionist _____ argued that Americans were members of a God-favored race destined to lead the world.

4. American Minister John L. Stevens ordered the marines to assist American rebels in their 1893 revolt against the native government in _____.

5. In 1899, the United States and Germany divided up the _____ Islands.

6. One of the foremost champions of an expanded American navy was President Harrison's secretary of the navy from 1889 to 1893, _____.

7. The "yellow press," led by circulation-hungry New York City newspaper publishers _____ and _____, published and printed sensationalistic stories of Spanish atrocities in Cuba, fueling Americans' desire for war.

8. On May 1, 1898, the American fleet under Commodore _____ easily crushed the Spanish fleet in Manila Bay.

9. Prominent industrialist and anti-imperialist _____ offered to buy Filipino independence with a personal check for $20 million.

10. A public health campaign headed by United States army surgeon _____ wiped out yellow fever in Cuba.

TRUE/FALSE

Mark the following statements either T (True) or F (False)

_____1. Theodore Roosevelt felt that an occasional war was necessary for the United States to prove its power and test the national spirit.

_____2. American businesspeople generally opposed United States acquisition of overseas colonies for fear that foreign products would undercut American prices.

_____3. Secretary of State James G. Blaine negotiated reciprocity treaties with Latin American countries in hopes of diverting their trade from Europe to the United States.

_____4. As president, Grover Cleveland consistently opposed an imperialistic policy for the United States.

_____5. A "fact-finding mission" sponsored by President McKinley in mid-1897 revealed that the press had greatly exaggerated the extent of problems in Cuba.

_____6. Arguing that reporters should only report and not influence events, New York Journal editor William Randolph Hearst opposed direct United States intervention on behalf of jailed Cuban revolutionary Evangelina Cisneros.

_____7. The Spanish American War was inevitable, given Spain's intransigence in refusing to consider any negotiation of the Cuban issue.

_____8. Racial theories of the latter nineteenth century contributed to racial harmony and understanding within the United States, easing the burdens of discrimination and segregation suffered by African Americans.

_____9. Riding a wave of patriotism and prosperity in 1900, McKinley defeated Bryan for president in a rematch election by an even larger margin than in 1896.

_____10. American proclamation, and lack of military enforcement, of the Open Door policy in China would lead to later controversy between the United State and Japan.

MULTIPLE CHOICE

Circle the one alternative that *best* completes the statement or answers the question.

1. During the early nineteenth century, some Americans urged abolition of the foreign service because
   a. our friendship with powerful Britain rendered the service unnecessary.
   b. there existed a shortage of candidates willing to enter the diplomatic field.
   c. the profession itself stirred dangers of entanglement in world struggles.
   d. American policy was too vulnerable to the whims of an uninformed electorate.

2. Proponents in favor of overseas expansion by the United States in the latter part of the nineteenth century argued that
   a. increasing American production necessitated the acquisition of additional markets.
   b. a worldwide scramble for empire might eliminate American opportunities for growth.
   c. it was our duty to extend civilization and Christianity to less privileged peoples.
   d. all of the above

3. The Inter-American Conference held in 1889 provided for the
   a. automatic arbitration of disputes in the Western Hemisphere.
   b. union of the United States and Latin America in a customs-free trade partnership.
   c. exchange of political, scientific, and cultural information among member nations.
   d. all of the above

4. The United States reasserted the Monroe Doctrine as a foreign policy by
   a. negotiating reciprocity treaties with the nations of Latin America.
   b. insisting that Britain submit its dispute with Venezuela over the boundary of British Guiana to United States arbitration.
   c. insisting that Britain pay the United States for damages caused by Confederate raiders built and outfitted in British shipyards during the Civil War.
   d. entering the Spanish-American War on behalf of Cuban independence.

5. Hawaii was annexed to the United States when
   a. a treaty was negotiated with the islands in 1875.
   b. American residents revolted in 1893 and formed a republic.
   c. President Cleveland served his second term as president.
   d. a joint resolution was passed by Congress during the Spanish-American War.

6. Military strategist and historian Alfred Thayer Mahan advocated an American policy of
   a. increasing imports of agricultural and manufactured goods.
   b. constructing railroads in Central and South America.
   c. expanding the nation's merchant marine and navy.
   d. all of the above

7. The appearance of American newspaper empires in the 1890s occurred because of
   a. the growing market of literate, urban readers.
   b. technological improvement in the presentation and dissemination of information.
   c. the adoption of "yellow journalism" techniques in stressing the sensational.
   d. all of the above

8. President Grover Cleveland responded to Cuba's war against Spain by
   a. supporting U.S. annexation of Cuba.
   b. offering to mediate the struggle.
   c. urging U.S. intervention in the war on Cuba's behalf.
   d. favoring recognition of Cuban independence.

9. In 1898, the American battleship *Maine* was
   a. sent to Manila as a gesture of strength and goodwill.
   b. captured by Spanish authorities in Havana.
   c. probably sunk as a result of an accidental internal explosion.
   d. sabotaged by Cuban revolutionaries.

10. In leading the country toward war, McKinley might properly be labeled a
    a. weak and indecisive president.
    b. victim of the war hysteria sweeping the country.
    c. wily manipulator for imperial gains.
    d. moderate in weighing both American interests and international considerations.

11. During the Spanish-American War, African American soldiers
    a. played a major role in the Cuban campaign.
    b. were utilized only in back-up and support positions.
    c. encountered little or no discrimination during training at home.
    d. refused to volunteer for military actions.

12. The Spanish-American War resulted in a
    a. long and costly military effort for the United States.
    b. sharp sense among Americans of deception and betrayal by their government.
    c. series of particularly embarrassing American naval defeats.
    d. greater loss of American lives to tropical diseases than battle.

13. Many anti-imperialists opposed American annexation of the Philippines because they feared that
    a. too many uneducated Filipinos would vote.
    b. defense of the territory might lead us into war.
    c. too many Americans would move to the islands.
    d. expanded trade in the Philippines would hurt our trade with China.

14. The Filipinos
    a. cooperated with Americans to drive the Spanish from their islands.
    b. willingly accepted American rule upon defeat of the Spanish.
    c. were granted independence by the United States in 1901.
    d. rejected suggested improvements offered by the Taft Commission for the Philippines.

15. United States Secretary of State John Hay's Open Door policy
    a. provoked the Boxer Rebellion of Chinese nationalists intent on ridding their country of foreign influences.
    b. called for China to grant the United States a sphere of influence with exclusive mining concessions.
    c. demanded the elimination of excessive Chinese tariffs and trade restrictions.
    d. guarded against the partition of China into foreign colonies and the consequent loss of American trading opportunities.

THOUGHT QUESTIONS

To check your understanding of the key issues of this period, solve the following problems:

1. What factors of the latter part of the nineteenth century contributed to an increasing interest by Americans in events abroad, preparing them for a larger role in the world?

2. Discuss the underlying as well as the immediate causes of the Spanish-American War. Why did John Hay refer to the conflict as "a splendid little war"?

3. Detail the arguments presented by American anti-imperialists against ratification of the Treaty of Paris in 1898–1899. Why did they fail?

4. The author notes that "historians rarely write of the Philippine-American War." Speculate on why this is so. Does the Philippine-American War seem similar to any other American war? Explain.

5. Did the United States Constitution "follow the flag" into American territories? Did Cuba win her independence following the Spanish–American War?

6. Explain the concept of the Open Door policy in China. Would it prove to be a successful policy for the United States?

CHAPTER 22

THE PROGRESSIVE ERA

SUMMARY
In late 1902, writers for *McClure's Magazine* introduced a new type of journalism, investigating and exposing the problems caused by rapid industrialization and urbanization. These journalists, dubbed "muckrakers" by Theodore Roosevelt, contributed to a broad reform movement call progressivism. From the mid-1890s through World War I, progressives challenged the status quo and sought changes in the nation's society, politics, economy, culture, and environment.

THE CHANGING FACE OF INDUSTRIALISM
In spite of persistent problems of poverty, disease, and racism, a new century and generally improved economic conditions brought a sense of optimism to Americans. The emergence of mammoth business enterprises from 1895 to 1915 led to inevitable changes in managerial attitudes, business organization, and worker roles.

The Innovative Model T
In 1913, Henry Ford established a moving assembly line to mass produce his standard automobile, the Model T. By dramatically reducing the time and costs of production, Ford managed to lower prices and expand sales and profits.

The Burgeoning Trusts
Standard Oil began a national trend among American big businesses toward oligopoly by swallowing up smaller competitors. By 1909, nearly one-third of the nation's manufactured goods were produced by only one percent of the industrial companies. Massive business mergers and reorganizations touched off a national debate over what the national government could or should do about the trusts. Many progressives as well as business leaders generally favored moderate reforms that would promote economic progress while protecting private property.

Managing the Machines
Assembly line production caused management to focus on speed and product rather than on the worker. Frederick Winslow Taylor introduced principles of "scientific management" to extract maximum efficiency. The industrial system promoted worker productivity, but jobs became increasingly monotonous and dangerous. A 1911 fire at the Triangle Shirtwaist Company in New York City killed 146 people and focused national attention on unsafe working conditions.

SOCIETY'S MASSES
The mass production of goods in America allowed greater consumption and required a larger work force. Women, African Americans, Mexican Americans, and immigrants played significant roles in the nation's economic expansion and sought to improve their individual as well as group conditions.

Better Times on the Farm
Farmers benefitted from greater production and expanding urban markets. Improved roads and mail service diminished rural isolation and brought farmers into the larger society. While rates of farm tenancy increased, especially in the South, successful efforts began to eliminate "farm-bred" diseases.

Women at Work
In 1900, one-fifth of all adult women worked, but most earned only meager wages. Continuing use of child labor provoked public indignation and led women reformers to lobby for federal protection of maternal and infant health.

The Niagara Movement and the NAACP
Progressive reforms seemed barely to touch the lives of African Americans. Most continued to labor in the cotton fields or in unskilled jobs. Few belonged to unions, obtained adequate education, or earned pay equal to that of white workers in the same jobs. African American leader W. E. B. Du Bois rejected the gradualist approach urged by Booker T. Washington and began the Niagara movement for racial justice and equality, resulting in the creation of the National Association for the Advancement of Colored People (NAACP) in 1910. Despite limited gains, African Americans continued to experience violence, segregation, and discrimination.

"I Hear the Whistle": Immigrants in the Labor Force
The "new" immigration of southern and eastern Europeans continued in the early twentieth century. Employers used "Americanization" programs in attempts to fashion dutiful habits among foreign workers. After 1910, large numbers of Mexicans fled to the United States, transforming society in the Southwest. The increasing numbers of immigrants intensified nativist sentiments.

CONFLICT IN THE WORKPLACE
Long hours, low pay, and the impersonal and unsafe conditions of factory jobs led to an increase of worker strikes, absenteeism, and union membership. Mindful of workers' problems and fearful of potential violence, progressives urged labor reforms.

Organizing Labor
The most successful union, the American Federation of Labor (AFL), restricted membership to skilled male workers and limited its agenda to issues of wages and working conditions. The Women's Trade Union League (WTUL) led the effort to organize women workers and promote their interests. The militant Industrial Workers of the World (IWW) urged labor solidarity and called for social revolution.

Working with Workers
Some business leaders used violence and police action to keep workers in line. Others learned to consider workers' job satisfaction and safety as well as pay as means to promote productivity and improve public relations.

Amoskeag
A large New England textile company, Amoskeag suffered no worker strikes from 1885 to 1919. The key to industrial harmony seemed to be the company's paternal interest in employee welfare, exhibited by its provision of recreational, educational, and health services for its workers.

LIFE IN AMERICA, 1920
The quality of life improved significantly for many Americans between 1900 and 1920. With rising incomes and greater leisure time, a growing middle class could take advantage of new lifestyles, inventions, and forms of entertainment.

An Urban Nation
Due to medical advances and improved living conditions, average life expectancy for Americans increased dramatically. By 1920, fewer than one-half of all Americans lived in rural areas. Rising urban affluence led to outlying suburbs, and major cities used zoning as a technique to shape growth and, often, extend racial and ethnic segregation.

THE USES OF LEISURE
Changing work rules and increasing mechanization from 1890 to 1920 gradually allowed American workers greater leisure time for play and enjoyment of the arts. Mass entertainment consisted of sports events, vaudeville and, later, movies as well as phonograph records of the new types of music—ragtime, blues, and jazz. As audiences grew, entertainment became big business as well.

Experimentation in the Arts
In the fine arts, Americans sought new forms and styles of expression, reflecting the period's pervading call for change and progress. The nation's urban centers, especially New York City and Chicago, attracted painters, writers, poets, dancers, and musicians interested in artistic experimentation. These artists joined with a generation of people in the fields of politics, journalism, science, education, and a host of others in hopes of progressive change.

LEARNING OBJECTIVES

After mastering this chapter, you should be able to

1. Relate the purposes and results of "muckraking" to the broader movement of progressivism.

2. Discuss the factors which contributed to a progressive movement of reform from 1890 to 1920.

3. Explain the changes in American industrialism during the early twentieth century regarding management and organization.

4. Discuss the contributions made and benefits derived by women, African Americans, Mexican Americans, and immigrants to the nation's economic expansion during the Progressive Era.

5. Explain the origins and purposes of the Niagara movement and the National Association for the Advancement of Colored People (NAACP).

6. Examine the causes for and results of conflict in the industrial workplace.

7. Analyze the successes and failures of union activities during this era.

8. Discuss the new methods employed by industrialists to increase productivity, job safety, and worker satisfaction.

9. Explain how the effects of mass production and mass entertainment altered the lifestyles and tastes of Americans.

10. Describe the various types of experimentation in the fine arts in America during this era.

GLOSSARY

To build your social science vocabulary, familiarize yourself with the following terms:

1. **muckrakers** those who search out and publicly expose real or apparent misconduct of prominent figures. "Readers were enthralled, and articles and books by other muckrakers . . . spread swiftly."

2. **burgeoning** expanding; flourishing. ". . . Americans took pride in teeming cities, burgeoning corporations, and other marks of the mass society."

3. **oligopoly** control of an industry or service by a few powerful companies. "The result was not monopoly, but oligopoly—control of a commodity or service by a small number of large, powerful companies."

4. **finance capitalists** investors or business people who subsidize capitalist endeavors. ". . . finance capitalists like J. P. Morgan tended to replace the industrial capitalists of an earlier era."

5. **hallmark** a conspicuous indication of the character or quality of something. "Their efforts . . . became another important hallmark of the Progressive Era."

6. **tenancy** the occupancy of lands by paying rent to the owner. "Tenancy grew from one-quarter of all farms in 1880 to more than one-third in 1910."

7. **grandfather clause** a discriminatory clause aimed at African Americans in the constitutions of several southern states prior to 1915, exempting from voting restrictions descendants of persons who were registered voters before 1867. "In *Guinn v. United States* (1915), the Supreme Court overturned a 'grandfather clause' . . . in Oklahoma."

8. **stereotypes** common or standard impressions usually representing an oversimplified opinion, feeling, or judgment. "Immigration patterns often departed from traditional stereotypes."

9. **barrios** ethnic grouping in a certain part of a town or city by Latin Americans. "Like other immigrant groups, they also formed enclaves in the cities, *barrios*. . . ."

10. **productivity** a measure of the efficiency of production, usually expressed in terms of output per man-hour. ". . . labor productivity dropped ten percent between 1915 and 1918. . . ."

11. **arbitration** process by which the parties to a dispute submit their differences to the judgment of an impartial third party. ". . . the important Hart, Schaffner agreement, which created an arbitration committee. . . ."

12. **bureaucratic** characterized by a narrow, rigid, formal routine. "As businesses grew in size, they also grew more bureaucratic. . . ."

13. **utopian** characterized by impossibly ideal or perfect conditions. "At first scornful of the 'utopian' plan, business leaders across the country soon copied it. . . ."

14. **zoning** to set aside areas of a city by legal restriction for purposes of business, residential, or entertainment needs. "Zoning ordered city development. . . ."

15. **avant garde** characterized by the creation or application of new or experimental ideas, especially in the arts. "Defiantly avant garde, they shook off convention and experimented with new forms."

IDENTIFICATION

Briefly identify the meaning and significance of the following terms.

1. Lincoln Steffens _____

_____

2. progressivism _____
_____

3. Henry Ford _____
_____

4. Frederick Winslow Taylor _____
_____

5. Triangle Shirtwaist Company fire _____
_____

6. National Association for the Advancement of Colored People (NAACP) _____
_____

7. "new" immigration _____
_____

8. Women's Trade Union League (WTUL) _____
_____

9. Amoskeag _____
_____

10. New York Armory show _____
_____

MATCHING

A. Match the following with the appropriate description.

_____ 1. Ida Tarbell   **a**. social worker who headed the Children's Bureau within the Bureau of Labor

____ 2. Margaret Sanger	b. muckraking author of the "History of the Standard Oil Company"

____ 3. Grace Abbott	c. fiery young radical who joined the Industrial Workers of the World (IWW) as a teenager

____ 4. Elizabeth Gurley Flynn	d. outspoken social reformer and head of the birth control movement

____ 5. Margaret Dreier Robins	e. one of the founding members of the National Association for the Advancement of Colored People (NAACP)

f. organizer of the influential Women's Trade Union League (WTUL)

B. Match the following entertainers with the appropriate description.

____ 1. D. W. Griffith	a. "Empress of the Blues," she made over eighty records that sold nearly ten million copies

____ 2. Florenz Ziegfeld	b. talented and creative director, he produced the nation's first movie spectacular, *The Birth of a Nation* in 1915

____ 3. Irving Berlin	c. classical dancer, she rejected traditional ballet steps to stress improvisation, emotion, and the human form

____ 4. Bessie Smith	d. producer of the "Follies," the peak of vaudeville entertainment

____ 5. Isadora Duncan	e. Russian immigrant composer, he set off a nationwide dance craze with his "Alexander's Ragtime Band" in 1911

f. composer and businessman, he joined with others to form the American Society of Composers, Authors, and Publishers (ASCAP) to protect musical rights and royalties

COMPLETION

Answer the question or complete the statement by filling in the blanks with the correct word or words.

1. The term "muckraker" was coined by _____ in 1906 to describe the practice of exposing the corruption of public and prominent figures.

2. The federal government authorized partial national funding for roadbuilding in states which established highway departments in the _____ Act of 1916.

3. An industrial research laboratory where scientists and engineers developed new products was first established by _____ in 1900.

4. The Rockefeller Sanitary Commission began a campaign in 1909 that eventually wiped out the _____ disease in rural America.

5. Rejecting the gradualist approach toward civil rights for African Americans, _____ provided inspiration for the Niagara movement.

6. Labor agents, called _____ among the Italians, Greeks, and Syrians, recruited immigrant workers, found them jobs, and deducted a fee from their wages.

7. Designed to curtail immigration from southern and eastern Europe, Congress passed a _____ requirement over President Wilson's veto in 1917.

8. A militant labor union, the _____, attracted the support of immigrant factory workers, migrant farm laborers, loggers, and miners.

9. New Orleans musicians Charles "Buddy" Bolden, Ferdinand "Jelly Roll" Morton, and Louis Armstrong helped popularize the new improvisational musical form called _____.

10. During the Progressive Era, a new group of realistic artists in America, known to their critics as the _____, painted scenes of American slums and tenements.

TRUE/FALSE

Mark the following statements either T (True) or F (False)

_____ 1. In responding to the disorder created by industrialization and urbanization, progressives remained hopeful of positive change.

_____ 2. Henry Ford applied the vital economic lesson that a larger unit profit on a smaller number of sales meant grater profits.

_____ 3. Progressive reformers unanimously agreed that business trusts should be broken up to restore individual opportunity and prevent price manipulations.

_____ 4. From 1900 to 1920 in the United States, the divorce rate dropped and the birth rate soared.

_____ 5. To discuss their campaign for civil rights in 1905, African American leaders had to meet on the Canadian side of Niagara Falls because no hotel on the American side would take them.

_____ 6. Mexican Americans significantly contributed to the economic development of the American Southwest.

_____ 7. Industrial psychologists argued that "time and motion" efficiency studies had to be complemented with consideration of worker satisfaction to improve productivity./

_____ 8. The Women's Trade Union League attracted substantial numbers of members but exerted relatively little influence in the promotion of women's rights.

_____ 9. The introduction of zoning laws tended to enforce racial and ethnic segregation in American cities.

_____ 10. The 1913 art show of European Post-Impressionists at the New York Armory was hailed by critics for the realistic presentations of ordinary people and familiar scenes.

MULTIPLE CHOICE

Circle the one alternative that *best* completes the statement or answers the question.

1. Which of the following topics investigated by progressive muckrakers is accurately linked with its author?
    a. urban corruption and Ida Tarbell
    b. industrial abuses and David Graham Phillips
    c. poisonous drugs and Lincoln Steffens
    d. unsanitary meatpacking and Upton Sinclair

2. According to Henry Ford, the key to "democratizing" the automobile was
    a. applying the principles of scientific management.
    b. mass production through a continuous assembly-line process.
    c. increasing workers' wages to $5 per day.
    d. granting workers' demands for an eight-hour workday.

3. The debate between progressives and business leaders over trusts
   a. represented a simple contest between high-minded reformers and greedy businesspeople.
   b. involved all progressives in a national attempt to break up big business.
   c. led businesspeople to oppose virtually all government attempts to regulate the economy.
   d. often found both groups in agreement on fundamental principles.

4. Frederick W. Taylor believed that
   a. machines would end the domination of well-paid craftspeople.
   b. the assembly line would dehumanize workers and damage productivity.
   c. workers should have the unrestricted right to organize.
   d. management should take responsibility for job-related knowledge and enforce its control of the workplace.

5. The Triangle Shirtwaist Company disaster in 1911 called national attention to
   a. militant labor strikes, which seemed to threaten a national revolution.
   b. inadequate regulation of railroads and public transportation.
   c. unsafe and oppressive working conditions in New York factories.
   d. overcrowded residential conditions in New York's Lower East Side.

6. In comparison to 1890, American farmers by 1920
   a. lived in greated isolation from urban society.
   b. had increased in terms of numbers and percentage of the total population.
   c. benefitted from greater production and expanded markets.
   d. suffered from greater incidence of "farm-bred" diseases.

7. Most women workers of the early twentieth century
   a. earned minimum standards of wages in unskilled jobs.
   b. possessed the same education and job skills as their male counterparts.
   c. attained managerial or professional positions.
   d. tended to be married rather than single.

8. A notable victory for the NAACP during the Progressive Era occurred when the Supreme Court outlawed
   a. segregation in public schools.
   b. use of a "grandfather clause" in Oklahoma.
   c. discriminatory employment practices in industry.
   d. the poll tax as a voting restriction.

9. Chinese Americans differed from other immigrant groups coming to America during the Progressive Era in that they
   a. intended to remain and establish permanent homes.
   b. declined rather than increased in numbers due to exclusionary laws.
   c. were more likely to be female rather than male.
   d. worked hard to adopt American rather than maintain traditional Chinese customs.

10. Immigrants from Mexico to the United States
    a. arrived in increasing numbers after revolution there in 1910 forced many to flee.
    b. typically came from the lower classes, eager to escape poverty and violence at home.
    c. contributed significantly to the building of highways and railroads in the Southwest.
    d. all of the above

11. The key to success for the American Federation of Labor (AFL) in the early twentieth century was the union's
    a. acceptance for membership of all industrial workers.
    b. refusal to engage in strikes at the local level.
    c. limited membership and a concentration on basic issues.
    d. ideological support for labor solidarity and ultimate social revolution.

12. The primary objective of the Industrial Workers of the World (IWW) was to
    a. provide education and "Americanization" for foreign workers.
    b. overthrow the capitalist system.
    c. increase workers' wages and reduce their hours.
    d. convince politicians of the need for protective legislation.

13. In the important Hart, Shaffner agreement, the Women's Trade Union League (WTUL) gained for striking women workers
    a. substantial wage increases.
    b. drastic reduction in work hours.
    c. the right of collective bargaining.
    d. all of the above

14. From 1900 to 1920 in the United States, the
    a. life expectancy for most Americans increased.
    b. farm population significantly increased.
    c. incidence of heart disease and cancer declined.
    d. zoning of American cities reduced patterns of racial segregation.

15. Concerning the fine arts, which of the following trends marked the Progressive Era in America?
    a. Classical ballet steps were emphasized in dance.
    b. Traditional meter and rhyme were rejected as artificial constraints in poetry.
    c. Painting was romanticized and impressionistic.
    d. Americans rejected such crass musical forms as ragtime, blues, and jazz.

THOUGHT QUESTIONS

To check your understanding of the key issues of this period, solve the following problems:

1. What factors combined to create the Progressive movement for reform during the late nineteenth and early twentieth centuries?

2. Discuss the changes in managerial attitudes, business organization, and industrial worker roles during the early twentieth century.

3. Explain the conditions that prompted formation of the National Association for the Advancement of Colored People (NAACP). Evaluate its success during the Progressive Era.

4. Examine the causes for conflict in the industrial workplace from 1900 to 1920. How did workers and managers respond?

5. Was life in America "better" in 1920 than it had been in 1900? Explain.

CHAPTER 23

FROM ROOSEVELT TO WILSON IN THE AGE OF PROGRESSIVISM

SUMMARY
Despite trying to continue with Roosevelt's basic policies and directions, Taft's presidency was far from smooth, and a bitter rift developed between the two men and within their party.

THE SPIRIT OF PROGRESSIVISM
Despite philosophical differences, progressives held to several basic tenets. Being optimistic about human nature, they sought to humanize and regulate big business. Progressives believed in the necessity of educated intervention in people's lives and an active role by all levels of government to manifest reform. They believed in reforming the environment through scientific and moral approaches.

The Rise of the Professions
Between 1890 and 1920, a large number of national professional societies of accountants, architects, doctors, lawyers, etc. were formed. These new professionals formed a new active and assertive middle class dedicated not only to improving their respective professions, but also to bettering living conditions on all levels of society.

The Social-Justice Movement
Groups of concerned professionals brought pressure on cities and businesses to dramatically improve conditions. These social workers collected data on urban conditions, wrote books and pamphlets, and sought recognition as a distinct field within the social sciences.

The Purity Crusade
Many reform-conscious women dedicated themselves to the crusade to abolish alcohol and its evils from American life. Promoted by superb organizational efforts under the Women's Christian Temperance Union and the Anti-Saloon League, these reformers succeeded in winning passage of the Prohibition Amendment (18th) to the U.S. Constitution.

Woman Suffrage, Woman's Rights
With more women now college educated and becoming reform conscious, numerous organizations were started to promote the rights and welfare of American women. After long delays, the suffragists succeeded in gaining passage of the Nineteenth Amendment. Women progressives also worked to regulate child and female labor.

A Ferment of Ideas
Stressing environmentalism and a more pragmatic approach to knowledge, a new generation of thinkers demanded reforms. William James introduced pragmatism while John Dewey pioneered a revolution in education. Thorstein Veblen attacked the disorder in business and industry. Louis Brandeis fought corporate abuses and political corruption. Socialists led by Eugene Debs attacked the abuses of capitalism and formed the Socialist party of America.

REFORM IN THE CITIES AND STATES

Interest Groups and the Decline of Popular Politics
Due to various factors, voter turnout dropped sharply in the quarter century after 1900. Many people turned to interest groups and professional and trade associations to promote their respective concerns.

Reform in the Cities
Stressing efficiency and results, substantial reform movements within city governments spread across the nation. Using new corps of experts, city officials constructed model governments and pushed through scientifically based policies. Galveston, Texas, and Cleveland, Ohio, were among the cities which implemented new policies and regulation of corrupt practices.

Action in the States
The most famous reformgovernor of the progressive era was Robert La Follette of Wisconsin. Under the "Wisconsin Idea," LaFollette improved education and workers' compensation, lowered railroad rates, and brought about the first state income tax.

THE REPUBLICAN ROOSEVELT
As McKinley's successor, Roosevelt brought a new spirit of enthusiasm and aggressiveness to the presidency. Early in his administration, Roosevelt appeared to support racial progress, but later retreated in the face of growing criticism.

Busting the Trusts
Distinguishing between "good" and "bad" trusts, Roosevelt sought to protect the former and regulate the latter. To regulate corporations, Congress created the Department of Commerce and Labor with a Bureau of Corporations. The president also pursued regulation through antitrust suits, most notably against J.P. Morgan's Northern Securities Company and the American Tobacco Company.

"Square Deal" in the Coalfields
Viewing the federal government as an impartial "broker" between labor and management, Roosevelt pressured the coal companies to settle their differences with the United Mine Workers or face executive intervention.

Another Term
Easily winning in his bid for reelection, Roosevelt moved into other areas of reform in his second term. The powers of the Interstate Commerce Commission were strengthened by passage of the Hepburn Act. The Meat Inspection Act and the Pure Food and Drug Act answered the public demand for regulation of the food and drug industry. The president significantly broadened the concept and policy of conservation of natural resources.

THE ORDEAL OF WILLIAM HOWARD TAFT
William Howard Taft, who unlike his predecessor disdained the limelight, succeeded Roosevelt as president in 1908. Lacking Roosevelt's faith in the power of the federal government to intercede in the public arena, Taft's years in the White House were not happy.

Party Insurgency
Failing to heal the Republican party rift over the tariff, Taft accepted the compromise bill, the Payne-Aldrich Act, which angered progressives. Discredited in their eyes, he leaned more on party conservatives.

The Ballinger-Pinchot Affair
Taft supported the attempt by Secretary of Interior Ballinger to sell a million acres of public land to a syndicate headed by J.P. Morgan. Gifford Pinchot was fired from the Forest Service because of his protests, and conservationists were furious.

Taft's Final Years
The Mann-Elkins Act, which further strengthened the Interstate Commerce Commission, and the Sixteenth Amendment, authorizing income taxes, were positive accomplishments of an otherwise divisive administration. Supporting competition within the business world and using the "rule of reason" against unfair trade practices by corporations, Taft further alienated himself from his former mentor Roosevelt. The former president decided to seek the presidency in 1912.

Differing Philosophies in the Election of 1912
Taft controlled the party machinery and captured the Republican nomination. Roosevelt, promoting his program, the New Nationalism, organized the progressive Republicans under his banner. But the Democrats, in nominating the scholarly Governor Woodrow Wilson and in taking advantage of the wounded Republican party, captured the presidency.

WOODROW WILSON'S NEW FREEDOM
Wilson announced his New Freedom program and called for a return to business competition and an end to special privilege.

The New Freedom in Action
Despite his lack of political experience, Wilson seized the progressive initiative and pushed landmark successes through Congress. The Underwood Tariff substantially reduced rates and levied a modest income tax. The Federal Reserve Act centralized banking and created the Federal

Reserve Board to regulate interest rates and the money supply. The Clayton Antitrust Act brought about much needed improvements in regulating trusts, outlawed interlocking directorates, and created the Federal Trade Commission.

Retreat and Advance

Despite measured successes in labor, child labor, and farming reforms, Wilson's New Freedom was a disappointment to women and African Americans. In 1916, Wilson again pushed for a multitude of reforms. Included were the Federal Farm Loan Act; the Adamson Act, the Keating-Owen child labor law and support for women's suffrage. After 1916, Wilson accepted much of the New Nationalism supporting greater federal power and regulation. As America neared military intervention in the war in Europe, the reform experiment came to an end.

LEARNING OBJECTIVES

After mastering this chapter, you should be able to

1. Determine specifically what progressivism meant at the city and the state level (especially the reform efforts under La Follette).

2. Explain what Roosevelt meant by the "bully pulpit" and how he applied this to his administration.

3. Analyze Roosevelt's attitude toward the trusts and the role of the federal government in trade issues and labor disputes.

4. Summarize the progressive measures of the Roosevelt presidency, with emphasis on railroad regulation, food and drug regulation, and conservation.

5. Contrast Taft's approach to executive leadership with Roosevelt's, specifying their different attitudes toward reform.

6. Determine the issues that adversely affected Taft's relationship with Progressives and influenced his downfall in 1912.

7. Determine the political effects of Taft's handling of the Ballinger-Pinchot affair and his support for the Payne-Aldrich Tariff.

8. Reveal the specific disappointments of African Americans, farmers, and women to Wilson's first-term policies.

9. List and briefly explain the major reforms of Wilson's second term.

10. Discuss the six or so major characteristics that defined and shaped progressivism.

11. Examine the participation of women in the social-justice movement and in the efforts to bring about prohibition and women's suffrage.

12. Summarize the impact of new ideas such as pragmatism and environmentalism.

13. Discuss the issues involved and the reasons for Wilson's success in the 1912 election.

14. Define the basic theory and attitude behind Wilson's New Freedom.

15. Outline the major components of the Underwood Tariff, the Federal Reserve Act, and the Clayton Antitrust Act.

GLOSSARY

To build your social science vocabulary, familiarize yourself with the following terms:

1. **peonage** a condition of compulsory servitude to a property holder or service because of a debt. "He denounced lynching and ordered the Justice Department to act against peonage."

2. **protectionist** one who believes in high protective tariffs to shield domestic manufacturing. ." . . passed a bill providing for lower rates, but in the Senate, protectionists raised them."

3. **rule of reason** discretionary standard applied by the courts to determine whether a corporation is in violation of antitrust laws. ". . . established the 'rule of reason' which allowed the Court to determine whether a business was a 'reasonable' restraint on trade."

4. **interlocking directorates** companies that are united by common directors or trustees. ". . . through 'interlocking directorates,' controlled companies worth $22 billion. . . ."

5. **antitrust** of or relating to laws protecting industry and commerce from unfair or illegal business practices. "Taft thought the decisions gave the Court too much discretion, and he pushed ahead with the antitrust effort. . . ."

6. **suffragist** one who advocates the right of women to vote. "After three generations of suffragist efforts, the Nineteenth Amendment. . . ."

7. **workers' compensation** state laws that guarantee monetary compensation to workers injured on the job, paid in part or full by the employer. "Maryland passed the first workers' compensation law in 1902."

8. **referendum** a device (usually implemented at the state level) that allows voters to accept or reject an existing statute at the ballot box ". . . the referendum which allowed them to accept a law. . . ."

9. **conservationist** one who believes in preserving natural resources such as forests and wildlife. ". . . he established the first comprehensive national conservation policy."

10. **insurgency** an aggressive or rebellious attitude. ". . . there was growing party insurgency against high rates."

11. **pragmatism** the belief in that which is practical, measurable, or useful. "A new doctrine called pragmatism emerged in this ferment of ideas."

12. **progressivism** the movement for political, economic, and social reforms. "Finally, progressivism was distinctive because it touched virtually the whole nation."

13. **environmentalism** the belief that moral and intellectual differences between individuals or groups are largely shaped by environmental factors. ". . . a reform sociologist, called in *Sin and Society* (1907) for pure environmentalism."

14. **methodology** a set of methods or procedures for regulating a discipline. ". . . social workers discovered each other's efforts, shared methodology, . . . "

15. **anarchic** favoring the overthrow of political authority usually through random acts of terrorism. ". . . modern business was an anarchic struggle for profit."

IDENTIFICATION

Briefly identify the meaning and significance of the following terms.

1. Northern Securities Company _____

_____

2. Hepburn Act _____

_____

3. *The Jungle* _____

_____

4. Payne-Aldrich Act _____

_____

85

5. Ballinger-Pinchot controversy _____

_____

6. "Bull Moose" _____

_____

7. New Freedom _____

_____

8. American Medical Association (AMA) _____

_____

9. Women's Christian Temperance Union (WCTU) _____

_____

10. "Brandeis brief" _____

_____

MATCHING

A. Match the following public figures with the appropriate description.

_____1. Gifford Pinchot   **a**. progressive and first Jewish justice of the Supreme Court, appointed by Wilson

_____2. Upton Sinclair   **b**. leader of the NAACP who proposed a National Race Commission

_____3. Oswald Garrison Villard   **c**. conservation activist and head of the Forest Service under Roosevelt

_____4. Richard Ballinger   **d**. writer who exposed "hideous" conditions and practices within the meat-packing industry

_____5. Louis Brandeis   **e**. Taft's secretary of the interior who offered for sale a million acres of land to private concerns

                     f. reform governor of Wisconsin who campaigned for federal control of railroads

B. Match the following federal laws with the appropriate description.

_____1. Hepburn   **a.** established a sound, flexible currency system

_____2. Payne-Aldrich   **b.** outlawed interlocking directorates and unfair pricing policies

_____3. Underwood   **c.** lowered tariff rates an average of fifteen percent and authorized the first graduated income tax

_____4. Clayton   **d.** placed telephone and telegraph companies under ICC supervision

_____5. Mann-Elkins   **e.** empowered the ICC to fix reasonable maximum railroad rates

                                                f. conservative tariff law that discredited Taft and split the Republican party

COMPLETION

Answer the question or complete the statement by filling in the blanks with the correct word or words.

1. Because he believed that the presidency should be the primary institution for leadership and activity, Roosevelt called it the _____.

2. The executive department created by Roosevelt to investigate corporate and business practices was the Department of _____.

3. _____ strengthened the rate-making power of the ICC and increased membership of the ICC from five to seven.

4. Republican progressives and conservatives split after 1909, mainly because of congressional passage of the _____.

5. In the 1912 presidential campaign, Roosevelt called for a national approach to U.S. problems and called his program the _____.

6. The important tariff bill passed under President Wilson and the Democratic party was the _____.

7. Upton Sinclair's novel *The Jungle* caused Roosevelt to demand an investigation of the _____.

8. The social-justice movement had the most success in passing state laws which _____ for women.

9. For Woodrow Wilson, the most important issue of the 1912 campaign was an economy that was not planned, but was _____.

10. In pursuing reform objectives, the progressives displayed _____ about human nature.

TRUE/FALSE

Mark the following statements either T (True) or F (False).

_____1. "A crime equal to treason," as one newspaper put it, was Roosevelt's invitation to Booker T. Washington to lunch at the White House.

_____2. Roosevelt's intervention in the anthracite coal strike revealed his solid and consistent pro-labor stance in disputes against ownership.

_____3. Roosevelt believed that all trusts, whether good or bad, should be broken up.

_____4. Progressives tended to emphasize reforming the individual more than reforming the environment.

_____5. Women in the social-justice movement cared more about their moral influence than in influencing legislation.

_____6. Roosevelt brought suit against the Northern Securities Company because he felt it violated the Sherman Antitrust Act.

_____7. Under Daniel De Leon and Eugene Debs, American socialists supported a more militant brand of socialism than that which characterized European socialism.

_____8. The Payne-Aldrich Tariff was a victory for the free trade advocates.

_____9. The Federal Reserve Act was designed to blend public and private control of the banking system.

_____10. Historians now see progressivism as being successful in bringing disparate groups together in working for reform rather than competing against each other.

MULTIPLE CHOICE

Circle the one alternative that *best* completes the statement or answers the question.

1. According to Roosevelt, the role of the federal government in labor issues should be to
   a. pursue a middle ground to curb corporate or labor abuses.
   b. side with labor in practically all matters.
   c. support ownership unless it is in violation of the Sherman Act.
   d. remain completely outside or above the issue.

2. The most accurate statement revealing Roosevelt's attitude toward the trusts would be that
   a. some controls were necessary, but large-scale industrial growth and production were natural and beneficial.
   b. trusts represented the corporate abuses and worker exploitation by the "malefactors of great wealth."
   c. a return to smaller scale corporate development and increased competition among more producers was necessary.
   d. large trusts were desirable as long as the owners recognized the unqualified right of unions to organize and represent their workers.

3. The Hepburn Act
   a. created the Interstate Commerce Commission.
   b. placed the burden of proof of railroad company abuses upon the courts.
   c. established the Department of Commerce and the Bureau of Corporations.
   d. broadened the jurisdiction and increased the powers of the ICC, allowing it to establish maximum railroad rates.

4. Concerning reform, Taft differed from Roosevelt in that he
   a. believed the federal government should take responsibility for all social and economic reforms.
   b. saw the principal responsibility as lying with the states.
   c. distrusted the government's ability to impose reforms or improve individual behavior.
   d. thought the president should be a stern, aggressive executive and take charge when improvements were needed.

5. The result of the Payne-Aldrich Act in terms of political fallout was that
   a. the Republican party was perceived for the first time to oppose wholesale tariff reduction.
   b. the progressive Republicans were alienated from Taft and increasingly turned to Roosevelt for leadership.
   c. the power of "Uncle Joe" Cannon as Speaker of the House was strengthened, stifling further reform impetus.
   d. most congressional Democrats supported the act, improving the position and image of that party in future elections.

6. The New Nationalism supported
   a. a retreat from progressive reforms—a new conservatism in other words.
   b. stronger antitrust legislation to prevent large concentrations of labor and capital.
   c. a stronger president, efficiency in government and society, and additional reforms to protect workers, women, and children.
   d. significant tariff reduction and establishment of sound, flexible currency.

7. The two groups that were conspicuously ignored by Wilson's progressive reforms in his first term were
   a. labor and farmers.
   b. Jews and bankers.
   c. women and African Americans.
   d. income-tax supporters and downward tariff revision advocates.

8. The "Wisconsin Idea" under La Follette consisted of
   a. industrial commissions, improved education, public utility controls, and lowered railroad rates.
   b. the first statewide use of property taxes to fund new programs.
   c. the "busting" of large corporations that violated the public trust.
   d. lower taxes of all kinds.

9. Thorstein Veblen argued that
   a. socialism was the only cure for the extremely unfair economic conditions in America.
   b. reform was demanded in an economic system characterized by disorder.
   c. he existing high level of organization in the American economy could be copied and applied to other areas of American life.
   d. economic changes had not occurred as rapidly as social changes.

10. Wilson's position regarding the labor movement was that he supported
    a. retreat from the previous two administrations' policies of consideration for labor reforms.
    b. business over labor categorically.
    c. balance between business and labor, union recognition, and collective bargaining.
    d. the use of military force to quell labor disturbances rather than negotiations.

11. As the leading educational progressive, John Dewey stressed
    a. children's individual needs and capabilities and the changed social situation.
    b. rote memorization and authoritarian teaching methods.
    c. that education was directly related to inherited and racial factors.
    d. strict common standards that all students should meet.

12. Dr. Alice Hamilton was involved in the efforts to
    a. eradicate the evils of alcohol.
    b. educate prostitutes to the dehumanizing aspects of their trade.
    c. organize the American Medical Association.
    d. alert state leaders to the problems of occupational diseases.

13. Progressives were united in the faith that
    a. the rights of women and minorities were more important than other concerns.
    b. legislative reforms were usually inadequate in meeting the prominent needs for social change.
    c. humans possessed the capacity actually to achieve a better world.
    d. most reforms should be addressed at local and regional levels rather than national.

14. Wilson could be best described personally as
    a. slow and amiable.
    b. moralistic and prone to self-righteousness.
    c. practical and down-to-earth.
    d. personable and compromising.

15. In the 1910 congressional elections,
    a. Republicans lost control of House and Senate.
    b. most Republicans were reelected, indicating popular support for Taft's policies.
    c. most progressive candidates were defeated by conservatives.
    d. there was very little change in either Republican or Democratic membership.

THOUGHT QUESTIONS

To check your understanding of the key issues of this period, solve the following problems:

1. How would you explain Roosevelt's attitude toward trusts, the labor movement, and conservation?

2. Despite his good intentions and prior success as an administrator, Taft in his administration was plagued by problems and, as the public perceived, numerous failures. How do you account for this?

3. Wilson's administration revolutionized the role of the federal government in regulating banking, business, and trade. To what extent were the reforms of the New Freedom permanent, and to what extent do they affect American society today?

4. What problems were left unsolved or even unapproached by progressive reformers and progressive presidents?

5. What new view of government and its roles and responsibilities did most progressives have?

6. What basic views united progressives? Were progressives accurate in their appraisal of human nature?

7. How would you describe the conditions from which women suffered in the early twentieth century?

8. Roosevelt believed that the president should exhibit strong, active executive leadership as well as initiate reforms. How do you think his administration measured up to those standards?

CHAPTER 24

THE NATION AT WAR

SUMMARY
In 1915, the British steamship *Lusitania* was sunk by a German submarine off the coast of Ireland with 1200 fatalities. The tragedy embroiled the United States more deeply in the European crisis and, despite Wilson's commitment to peace and neutrality, America went to war in 1917.

A NEW WORLD POWER
After 1901, the United States was becoming much more involved through economic expansion in international issues. Policy making was left almost entirely to the president because most Americans paid little attention to foreign affairs.

"I Took the Canal Zone"
The strong desire for an isthmian canal to connect the two oceans led to a major departure in U.S.-Latin American relations. President Roosevelt, convinced that America should achieve a more active international status, intervened in affairs in Colombia-Panama to secure the canal zone, and in 1914, the canal was completed. The Hay-Bunau-Varilla Treaty gave the United States control of the canal zone and guaranteed the independence of Panama.

The Roosevelt Corollary
With American interests entrenched in the Caribbean, the president issued the Roosevelt Corollary to the Monroe Doctrine to allow for American intervention in Latin America when necessary.

Ventures in the Far East
In the Far East, Roosevelt sought to normalize relations with Japan after that rising power's military victory over Russia. In 1908, Roosevelt sent the enlarged naval fleet around the world, with a stop in Tokyo, as a show of strength.

Taft and Dollar Diplomacy
Under President Taft, American business and financial interests were extended abroad through "dollar diplomacy." Taft's initiatives in the Far East led to intense rivalry and increased tension with Japan.

FOREIGN POLICY UNDER WILSON
Confident of his own abilities and extremely idealistic, President Wilson foresaw a world freed from the threats of militarism, colonialism, and war.

Conducting Moral Diplomacy
President Wilson and Secretary of State William Jennings Bryan sought to apply a policy of human rights and national integrity to Latin America, but practical considerations softened Wilson's idealism.

Troubles across the Border
Revolution and lingering political instability caused Wilson to become embroiled in Mexican political turbulence. Incapable of bringing progressive reform or political stability and uncertain as to whom to support, Wilson used military intervention to track down the revolutionary Pancho Villa.

TOWARD WAR
The assassination of Austro-Hungarian Archduke Franz Ferdinand set into motion a chain of events which by August 1914 had brought the major European nations to war. Stunned as he was, Wilson called on the American people to remain impartial.

The Neutrality Policy
At the outset of war, Wilson envisioned the nation's role as that of a peacemaker and pillar of democracy. Americans were sharply divided in sentiment, but they accepted neutrality as the desirable course. A majority of Americans sympathized with the British and French and considered German aggression largely responsible for the war.

Freedom of the Seas
Despite occasional British blockades and German U-boat warfare, American goods flooded European ports especially in Britain and France, resulting in great profits at home and increasing commercial ties with the Allies.

The U-Boat Threat
Germany's use of a the dreaded submarines posed a direct threat to American shipping. The sinking of the Lusitania outraged Americans and forced President Wilson to pressure the German government. After the French steamer *Sussex* was sunk, German Kaiser Wilhelm issued a pledge promising that German submarines would only target enemy naval vessels.

"He Kept Us Out of War"
The "preparedness" advocates led by Theodore Roosevelt called for readiness in case of war and spoke out against pacifist sentiment in the country. Wilson ran successfully for reelection in 1916 against the Republican candidate Charles Evans Hughes. Winning by a very narrow margin, Wilson continued to pledge his commitment to peace.

The Final Months of Peace
In January 1917, Wilson called upon the European nations to submit to a "peace without victory" and a peace between equals, but renewed German submarine attacks severely threatened relations with the United States. Public indignation against Germany soared after the exposure of the Zimmermann telegram which encouraged a Mexican war against the U.S. and a Mexican-German

alliance in such a case. Prompted by continued sinkings of American ships, Wilson at last demanded military intervention.

OVER THERE
A wave of patriotism swept the country as hundreds of thousands of troops departed for Europe, and antiwar protest at home was crushed.

Mobilization
Wilson selected "Black Jack" Pershing to lead the American Expeditionary Force (AEF), and in May 1917, Congress passed the Selective Service Act which eventually drafted some two million men into the army.

War in the Trenches
A massive German offensive was launched in March 1918 against Western Europe, but the American supported Allied lines held, and in autumn, German forces were in headlong retreat. In November, Germany agreed to armistice terms. Within the month, Austria-Hungary, Turkey, and Bulgaria also were finished.

OVER HERE

The Conquest of Convictions
At home, the Committee on Public Information launched a propaganda campaign to evoke hatred for Germany. Wilson encouraged repression against antiwar sympathizers and enforced the Sedition Act against those who opposed the war effort. Despite opposition by Socialists and the I.W.W., organized repression hardly was justified. In 1918, Wilson who was fearful of the spread of Communist revolution from Russia, sent American troops into the Soviet Union, apparently to assist in dislodging the Bolshevik government. A postwar "Red Scare" of fear and hatred began at home.

A Bureaucratic War
The War Industries Board was established to oversee all aspects of industrial production. Herbert Hoover headed the Food Administration, and the Fuel Administration rationed coal and oil and imposed daylight savings time. Government involvement in American life had never been greater. Liberty bonds were sold, and taxes on individuals and corporations were boosted.

Labor in the War
The war fastened the partnership between labor and government, and union membership swelled to more than four million by 1919. The War Labor Board standardized wages and hours and protected the rights of workers to organize and collectively bargain. Women and African Americans found economic opportunities that had never before existed. Growing competition for jobs led to an increase in racial tensions. The United States emerged from the war as the greatest economic power in the world.

THE TREATY OF VERSAILLES
England and France reluctantly submitted to much of Wilson's idealistic plans for world peace.

A Peace at Paris
Wilson's lofty goals for a lasting peace included national self-determination in Europe and a League of Nations. Some of Wilson's important principles were sacrificed however as enormous reparations were heaped upon Germany, and the doctrine of self-determination was not always manifested in the legitimizing of new nations.

Rejection in the Senate
Because the treaty limited the power of Congress in some respects, senators with strong reservations were committed to oppose it. Wilson's refusal to budge on a few crucial points and his inability to campaign for it with his usual zest (he suffered a debilitating stroke) led to the treaty's final rejection. Republican Warren G. Harding's election in 1920 assured the final demise of the treaty and confirmed the nation's disillusionment with war and international commitment.

LEARNING OBJECTIVES

After mastering this chapter, you should be able to

1. Discuss the new role of the United States in Latin America and the various diplomatic approaches of Roosevelt, Taft, and Wilson.

2. List and explain the causes of the war in Europe and American reactions to the war.

3. Compare and contrast the arguments of the preparedness advocates and the pacifists.

4. Understand the factors that brought the U.S. into the war and the extent to which German belligerence in the North Atlantic was responsible.

5. Compare American military involvement and war-time losses with those of the major European nations.

6. Determine the reasons for the final military collapse of Germany.

7. Show the ways in which the wartime partnership between citizen and government worked and how the war affected women and African Americans.

8. Define the different goals of the victorious nations at the Paris Peace Conference, and explain how Wilson's goals were incorporated into the treaty.

9. Discuss the reasons for the failure of Wilsonian global idealism and the Versailles treaty.

10. Reflect on American disillusionment and the decline of the progressive spirit as the 1920s set in.

11. Describe the problems Wilson faced in Mexico and whether he handled them responsibly.

12. Specify the steps by which America mobilized for war.

13. Summarize the activities of the War Industries Board, the Committee on Public Information, and the War Labor Board.

14. Explain the concessions or sacrifices which Wilson had to make to the other European leaders regarding the peace structuring.

GLOSSARY

To build your social science vocabulary, familiarize yourself with the following terms:

1. **ultimatum** a proposition or demand with strong consequences for rejection. ". . . almost an ultimatum—warning Germany that the United States would view similar sinkings as 'deliberately unfriendly.'"

2. **protectorates** governments established by a major power over a dependent country. "Roosevelt also established protectorates in Cuba and Panama."

3. **status quo** the way things presently exist. ". . .in which they promised to maintain the status quo in the Pacific. . . ."

4. **militarism** a condition of aggressive military preparedness or strong military buildup. ". . . Wilson believed in a principled, ethical world in which militarism, colonialism, and war were brought under control."

5. **neutrality** a policy of remaining unaligned with any one side in an international conflict. "Wilson immediately proclaimed neutrality. . . ."

6. **jingoism** extreme nationalism, often to the point of belligerency or chauvinism. "'It is jingoism run stark mad. . . .'"

7. **pacifist** one who categorically opposes war. ". . . while pacifists denounced any attempt at military readiness."

8. **conscription** a forced contribution or draft of persons for military duty. "Wilson turned to conscription, which he felt was both efficient and democratic."

9. **self-determination** the right of a people or nation to choose their own form of government and leaders. ". . . and they were skeptical of the principle of self-determination."

10. **reparations** payments made for damages caused. ". . . it made Germany accept responsibility for the war and demanded enormous reparations. . . ."

11. **belligerent** warring or warlike. ". . . neutral countries were permitted to trade in nonmilitary goods with all belligerent countries."

12. **bellicose** inclined toward quarreling or aggressive arguments. "Bellicose as always, Teddy Roosevelt led the preparedness campaign."

13. **vigilantism** preparedness for emergency. "Vigilantism, sparked often by superpatriotism of a ruthless sort, flourished."

14. **assimilated** made similar or integrated. "Society assimilated some of the shifts, but social and economic tensions grew. . . ."

15. **arbitration** intervention by an impartial third party in disputes with the decision usually binding. "League members pledged to submit to arbitration every dispute. . . .

IDENTIFICATION

Briefly identify the meaning and significance of the following terms.

1. *Lusitania* _____

_____

2. Roosevelt Corollary _____

_____

3. *Sussex* pledge _____

_____

4. "dollar diplomacy" _____

_____

5. League of Nations _____

_____

6. Zimmermann telegram _____
_____

7. Bolshevik _____
_____

8. Sedition Act _____
_____

9. War Industries Board _____
_____

10. Fourteen Points _____
_____

MATCHING

A. Match the following diplomatic measures with the appropriate description.

_____ 1. Hay-Herrán Convention   **a**. recognized Japan's dominance over Korea in return for her agreement not to interfere in the Philippines

_____ 2. Hay-Bunau-Varilla Treaty   **b**. was convened by Roosevelt to end the war between Japan and Russia, from which Japan emerged as a major world power

_____ 3. Taft-Katsura Agreement   **c**. contained a promise by German government not to fire on nonmilitary ships in the North Atlantic

_____ 4. Portsmouth   **d**. in agreement with Colombia, gave the United States the right to dig an isthmian canal and a ninety-nine-year lease

_____ 5. *Sussex* pledge   **e**. granted American control over the Panama Canal Zone in return for U.S. guarantee of Panamanian independence

    f. increased American suspicion of German intervention in Mexico

B. Match the following public figures with the appropriate description.

_____ 1. George Creel

_____ 2. Bernard Baruch

_____ 3. Herbert Hoover

_____ 4. Eugene V. Debs

_____ 5. Harry A. Garfield

a. head of the wartime Fuel Administration who introduced daylight savings time

b. Socialist party leader who was imprisoned for denouncing capitalism and the war

c. head of the Food Administration who supplied food to American armies overseas

d. leader of the Committee on Public Information to publicize the war effort

e. businessperson who oversaw the War Industries Board, which determined manufacturing priorities

f. head of the War Labor Board, which standardized hours and wages

COMPLETION

Answer the question or complete the statement by filling in the blanks with the correct word or words.

1. The secretary of state who chose to resign rather than sign a note demanding certain pledges from Germany after the sinking of the Lusitania was _____.

2. To consolidate the country's new position in the Caribbean and to strengthen America's two-ocean navy, Roosevelt desired _____.

3. With the _____ the United States and Japan promised to maintain the status quo in the Pacific and support Chinese independence.

4. Rejecting "dollar diplomacy," Wilson initially intended to follow a course of _____ to settle international disputes by right rather than might.

5. The longtime president of Mexico who invited foreign investments into the Mexican economy was _____.

6. At the outbreak of war in Europe, Wilson proclaimed _____ and asked the American people to remain impartial in thought and action.

7. The new weapon that violated traditional rules of warfare and strained United States-German relations was the _____.

8. The issue that dominated the presidential election of 1916 was _____.

9. The Mexican leader whom Wilson refused to recognize, calling him instead "the butcher," was_____.

10. When DuBois spoke of blacks as being more proud and militant after the war, he used the term_____ to describe them.

TRUE/FALSE

Mark the following statements either T (True) or F (False).

_____1. The Hay-Pauncefote Treaty gave the United States and Britain joint ownership of the proposed isthmian canal.

_____2. The new approach to Latin American affairs promised by Wilson was to elevate human rights and national integrity.

_____3. Because the Philippines were strategically crucial to American interests in the Pacific, Congress decided to fortify the islands promptly after acquisition.

_____4. William Jennings Bryan was appointed secretary of state by Wilson primarily because of his previous experience in foreign affairs through the State Department.

_____5. "The dirty hunger for dollars" was to blame for the European war, according to multimillionaire Henry Ford.

_____6. Because he had fought so doggedly for neutrality, Wilson was able to sympathize with those Americans who opposed the U.S. entry into the war in 1917.

_____7. Because of the Zimmermann telegram and the possibility of war with Mexico as well as the universal hatred for Mexicans by southwestern Americans, Congress tightened immigration restrictions from south of the border after 1917.

_____8. The fact that most African Americans actively supported the war effort had a calming effect on racial tensions at home after the war.

_____9. Most Irish immigrants in the United States favored Germany in World War I even though Irish troops were fighting for the British.

_____ 10. Because of the almost universal hatred for the American Socialist party expressed during and after the Paris peace talks, the party became stronger.

MULTIPLE CHOICE

Circle the one alternative that *best* completes the statement or answers the question.

1. The Roosevelt Corollary
   a. promised an American empire in the Caribbean.
   b. warned European nations to eliminate all economic interests in Latin America.
   c. warned of American intervention in Latin American affairs when necessary.
   d. acquired Cuba for the United States as a territory.

2. The approach of President Taft toward foreign affairs was to
   a. increase military buildup and involvement.
   b. promote American financial and business interests.
   c. oppose all nondemocratic regimes.
   d. attract European capital and loans to Latin America.

3. According to Woodrow Wilson, the objectives and pursuits of the American people should be
   a. moral principle, preservation of peace, and extension of democracy.
   b. military power and increased armaments.
   c. material interests and "dollar diplomacy."
   d. overwhelming concern for domestic progressive issues to the sacrifice or preclusion of foreign problems.

4. One of the major reasons for the war in Europe in 1914 was
   a. the fear of Britain and France toward the rising power of Russia.
   b. the fear of creeping communist revolutions throughout Europe.
   c. the breakup of the Austro-Hungarian empire and the desire for additional territories by her southeastern European neighbors.
   d. a web of entangling alliances which could cause a local problem to escalate into a major war.

5. At the outset of the European war, most Americans
   a. accepted neutrality as advisable and moral.
   b. favored entering the war on the side of Britain and France.
   c. blamed Britain for the war because of its extensive imperial system.
   d. were unconcerned with events in Europe.

6. The preparedness advocates called for
   a. American entry into the war at any cost.
   b. naval destroyers to accompany merchant vessels across the North Atlantic.
   c. Roosevelt to run for the presidency in 1916.
   d. military readiness in case of war.

7. The Committee on Public Information was responsible for
   a. giving the American people clear and objective reasons why the United States was compelled to intervene in the war.
   b. distributing news items to the major daily papers and other media.
   c. using the arts, advertising, and film industries to publicize the war and launching a propaganda campaign to popularize the war effort against the barbaric Germans.
   d. keeping a watchful eye on antiwar sympathizers and publicly discrediting them.

8. The effect of the war on organized labor was to
   a. bring labor into partnership with the federal government and greatly increase union membership.
   b. allow the government to forbid strikes or work slowdowns.
   c. weaken labor because most workers were called into the armed forces.
   d. allow women to unionize on the same basis as men.

9. African American participation in the war could best be described in which of the following ways?
   a. African Americans were not allowed in the armed forces in any capacity.
   b. African Americans were enlisted in support and supply units but were not allowed in combat.
   c. More than forty thousand African Americans served in combat but were commonly discriminated against when they returned home.
   d. African Americans were fully integrated into the armed forces and treated the same as white troops for the most part.

10. Which of the following was not a major goal of Wilson's at the Paris Peace Conference?
    a. enforcement of enormous financial reparations upon the Germans
    b. national self-determination for European ethnic and nationalist groups
    c. a League of Nations to settle international disputes
    d. reduction of tensions through disarmament and establishment of free trade

11. The Hay-Bunau-Varilla Treaty granted
    a. the United States control of a canal zone through Panama.
    b. the United States and Britain joint ownership of the canal.
    c. the United States a ninety-nine year lease on a canal zone in return for payments to Colombia.
    d. Colombia preferential treatment in using the canal.

12. Most progressives in the United States believed that the European war was the result of
    a. the failure of international diplomacy.
    b. greed of financiers, munitions manufacturers, stockbrokers, and others eager for wartime profits.
    c. the lack of commitment on the part of European governments to liberal reforms.
    d. the absence of American leadership in encouraging other nations to establish their own progressive reform agendas.

13. The German policy that was most directly responsible for bringing the United States into the war was the
    a. support for Mexico with arms and money during the punitive expedition.
    b. decision to renew unrestricted submarine warfare in the North Atlantic against American vessels.
    c. sinking of the *Lusitania*.
    d. revelation of wartime objectives including territorial gains in Europe and Africa.

14. The key issue in the 1916 presidential campaign was
    a. that Wilson had kept us out of war and that Hughes was perceived to be more aggressive toward Germany.
    b. the proposed extension of suffrage to women.
    c. whether civil rights for African Americans would be included in the continued progressive agenda.
    d. whether we would eventually come into the European war on the side of Germany or on the side of Britain and France.

15. Wilson's attitude toward antiwar dissent after American entry was to
    a. tolerate it because of his own moral revulsion to war.
    b. crack down on superpatriotic vigilantism directed against antiwar sympathizers.
    c. encourage repression and humiliation of antiwar sympathizers.
    d. refuse to concern himself because of the greater importance of directing the war in Europe.

THOUGHT QUESTIONS

To check your understanding of the key issues of this period, solve the following problems:

1. Neutrality, although the United States policy for the first three years of the war in Europe, was not actually neutral. What were the problems in remaining neutral?

2. Several factors prompted U.S. entry into the war against Germany in 1917. What do you consider to be the most important reasons for intervention?

3. How did mobilization change the habits and patterns of American society at home? To what extent did the federal government become "big brother" to the economy during the war?

4. W. E. B. Du Bois spoke of a "New Negro" during the war years. How did the war change the expectations and directions of blacks in a still predominantly white-dominated society?

5. How did the war damage the progressive, humanitarian spirit in America? How did disillusionment affect the U.S. at home, as well as in its relations with other countries?

6. How would you compare the Latin American policies of Presidents Roosevelt and Wilson? What problems with Mexico did Wilson's attitude of condescension and morality create?

7. Wilson attempted to apply his lofty ideals of morality and self-determination to the world arena after the war. Why were his goals difficult to achieve, and why specifically did the Senate reject his treaty?

CHAPTER 25

TRANSITION TO MODERN AMERICA

SUMMARY
The 1920s were marked by rapid economic and urban growth, inspiring tensions as rural America resisted the ensuing changes.

THE SECOND INDUSTRIAL REVOLUTION
Based on mass production, the moving assembly line, and the marketing of consumer goods, the economy of the 1920s experienced phenomenal growth.

The Automobile Industry
The automobile industry, one of the most important of the 1920s, significantly changed American culture.

Patterns of Economic Growth
The corporation run by a professional manager dominated the businesses of the 1920s, and brought conformity.

Economic Weaknesses
Despite the progress, some elements of the economy fared poorly, notably farmers, union members, and minorities.

THE NEW URBAN CULTURE
Still another important feature of the 1920s was the rapid rise of the city and the consequent changes in society.

Women and the Family
Families changed as a result of falling birth rates, rising divorce rates, and the flowering feminist movement.

The Roaring Twenties
The cultural revolution also prompted the rise of organized crime, spectator sports, and a sexual revolution.

The Literary Flowering
Frustrated with the materialism of mass culture, many literary figures wrote scathing criticisms of this new era. Others lived in self-exile in Europe. African American authors in America, however, found energy and inspiration in the Harlem Renaissance.

THE RURAL COUNTERATTACK
Insecurity in the face of all this social upheaval caused rural and small-town America to react to the dominance of the city.

The "Red Scare"
Tradition-minded Americans feared the specter of bolshevism or anarchism and tried to eliminate radicalism from American life.

Prohibition
Many associated alcohol with alien cultures and the new urban ways and, therefore, tried to implement prohibition of the manufacture, sale, or transportation of alcoholic beverages.

The Ku Klux Klan
Some even joined such groups as the Ku Klux Klan in order to preserve what they thought was sacred and pure.

Immigration Restriction
Nativists successfully restricted foreign immigration.

The Fundamentalist Controversy
Some Americans found solace and security in supporting fundamentalist Christianity or in opposing theories of evolution being taught in the public schools.

POLITICS OF THE 1920S
Rural-urban tensions dominated the politics of the 1920s.

Harding, Coolidge, and Hoover
The Republicans dominated the White House with three popular presidents.

Republican Policies
In this era, the Republican party passed a program of higher tariffs, lower taxes, and spending cuts.

The Divided Democrats
The Democrats were divided on rural-urban issues, but were gaining strength among the new immigrant voters of the big cities.

The Election of 1928
The election of 1928 symbolized the decade, pitting Democrat Al Smith, a Catholic, urban, "wet" son of immigrants, against Republican Herbert Hoover, an old-stock, "dry" Protestant from Iowa. Hoover won easily and then presided over the worst depression in American history.

LEARNING OBJECTIVES

After mastering this chapter, you should be able to

1. Explain the elements of the economic changes of the 1920s.

2. List the weaknesses of the American economy in the 1920s.

3. Discuss the impact of the rise of the city.

4. Analyze the key elements of the literary movement of the 1920s.

5. Describe the main features of the rural reaction of the 1920s.

6. Outline the personalities and contributions of the key political figures of the 1920s.

7. Explain the failures and successes of the Democrats from 1920-1930.

8. Analyze the election of 1928.

9. Discuss the policies of the Republican party during the 1920s.

10. Describe the changes wrought in the American family in the 1920s.

GLOSSARY

To build your social science vocabulary, familiarize yourself with the following terms:

1. **gross national product** the total market value of all goods and services produced in a country during one year. "The gross national product rose by 40 percent."

2. **per capita** relating to any statistical measurement in which an aggregate is divided by the total population. ". . . per-capita income increased by 30 percent. . . ."

3. **oligopoly** market structures in which control is in the hands of a few companies. "The oligopoly in the automobile industry set an example for other areas."

4. **dialect** a regional version of a language. ". . . the advent of radio and films which promoted a standard national dialect. . . ."

5. **yellow-dog contract** an employment contract in which an employee disavows union membership. "Many businessmen used . . . 'yellow-dog' contracts . . . [to] deny workers the benefits of collective bargaining."

6. **metropolis** the principal city of a state or nation. "In the metropolis, life was different."

7. **tabloids** newspapers that exploit sex and violence for mass appeal. ". . . the new urban tabloids-led by the *New York Daily News*--delighted in telling their readers about love nests and kept women."

8. **expatriates** those who have left or been forced to leave their country. "Some fled to Europe to live as expatriates. . . ."

9. **paradox** something that seems illogical but is nonetheless true. ". . . there is a striking paradox about the literary flowering of the twenties."

10. **bigotry** the practice of stubborn attachment to racial hatred. ". . . symbolized the bigotry and intolerance that lasted through the twenties."

11. **bolshevism** principles of the Russian Communist Party. "The heightened nationalism of World War I . . . found a new target in bolshevism."

12. **nativism** policies and principles of groups in the United States that oppose open immigration, especially of non-Anglo-Saxon Protestants. ". . . the recurring demons of nativism and hatred. . . ."

13. **fundamentalist sect** a Christian denomination that believes in a literal interpretation of the Bible. ". . . aggressive fundamentalist sects . . . grew rapidly."

14. **ethnic** relating to a group with common culture or customs. ". . . especially among the ethnic groups in the cities."

15. **bloc** a collection of groups united to further a common cause. "The farm bloc supported the higher tariffs. . . ."

IDENTIFICATION

Briefly identify the meaning and significance of the following terms.

1. Model T _____

_____

2. Samuel Insull _____

_____

3. Nineteenth Amendment _____

_____

4. Al Capone _____

_____

5. Babe Ruth _____

_____

6. Ernest Hemingway _____

_____

7. Sacco and Vanzetti _____

_____

8. Scopes trial _____

_____

9. Teapot Dome _____

_____

10. Al Smith _____

_____

MATCHING

A. Match the following writers with the appropriate description.

_____ 1. Ezra Pound   **a.** newspaperman and literary critic who founded the *American Mercury*

_____ 2. T. S. Eliot	b. popular novelist who satirized small-town America in works such as Main Street

_____ 3. Ernest Hemingway	c. poet who wrote without rhyme or meter

_____ 4. F. Scott Fitzgerald	d. poet who emphasized the emptiness of modern civilization

_____ 5. Sinclair Lewis	e. writer who described the emptiness of American culture in works such as *The Great Gatsby*

	f. author who wrote in a clean, direct prose style about his own daring experiences

B. Match the following acts with the appropriate description.

_____ 1. Eighteenth Amendment	a. gave women the right to vote

_____ 2. Nineteenth Amendment	b. provided money for maternal and infant health care

_____ 3. Sheppard-Towner Act	c. proposed to raise tariffs to a highly protectionist level

_____ 4. National Origins Quota Act	d. prohibited the manufacture and sale of alcoholic beverage

_____ 5. Fordney-McCumber Act	e. implemented prohibition and defined an illegal beverage as any above one percent alcohol by volume

	f. limited immigration mainly to people from northwestern Europe

COMPLETION

Answer the question or complete the statement by filling in the blanks with the correct word or words.

1. Henry Ford first used the technique of mass production with a moving assembly line to produce the _____.

2. The promoter who aggressively controlled many power companies in the 1920s was _____.

3. In 1923, the National Woman's Party, led by Alice Paul, had the _____ introduced into Congress.

4. The man who completed the first solo flight of the Atlantic was _____.

5. An African American intellectual in New York's Harlem community and editor of *Crisis* was _____.

6. The African American literary movement of the 1920s was known as the _____.

7. The attorney general who led an attack on suspected anarchists and Communists in 1919 was _____.

8. The Chicago defense attorney who defended John T. Scopes was _____.

9. The corrupt official in the Teapot Dome scandal was Interior Secretary _____.

10. The Democratic candidate in the election of 1928 was _____.

TRUE/FALSE

Mark the following statements either T (True) or F (False).

_____1. Mass production was not an important factor in the consumer-goods revolution.

_____2. Wage increases easily kept pace with increases in labor productivity.

_____3. The economic growth of the 1920s was mostly the result of the work of many small firms.

_____4. Agriculture did not participate in the prosperity of the 1920s.

_____5. Some influential women's groups did not support the Equal Rights Amendment.

_____6. There was a drop in the birth rate in the 1920s.

_____7. The Palmer raids were successful because officials were careful to arrest only bona-fide Bolsheviks.

_____8. The tariff policies of the Republicans of the 1920s favored lowering rates on imported goods.

_____9. Republican policy of the 1920s advocated cutting taxes and government spending.

_____10. Republican presidents effectively cut the number of government bureaucrats in half during the 1920s.

MULTIPLE CHOICE

Circle the one alternative that *best* completes the statement or answers the question.

1. Which of the following was *not* an element of the economic changes of the 1920s?
   a. mass production
   b. moving assembly line
   c. high profits in agriculture
   d. consumer goods revolution

2. The new professional class of corporate managers was
   a. dependent on investment bankers.
   b. dedicated to preserving individual entrepreneurship.
   c. accountable only to other managers.
   d. indifferent to social responsibility.

3. The government passed immigration acts in the 1920s that
   a. increased Mexican immigration.
   b. reduced northern and western European immigration.
   c. increased southern and eastern European immigration.
   d. was generous, especially to Asiatics.

4. The consumer-oriented economy stressed
   a. marketing.
   b. chain stores.
   c. buying on time.
   d. all of the above

5. Organized labor
   a. lost many members in the 1920s.
   b. had aggressive leadership.
   c. had the strong support of the courts.
   d. all of the above

6. The American family in the 1920s experienced
   a. declining divorce rates.
   b. increasing birth rates.
   c. declining birth rates.
   d. a declining rate of working wives.

7. The election of Warren G. Harding in 1920 meant that
   a. business would have no power in Washington.
   b. morality would be paramount in the actions of the new president.
   c. reform was not as popular as it had been.
   d. an increase in social and political reform.

8. The end of the Red Scare came about as a result of
   a. the acquittal of Sacco and Vanzetti.
   b. its own extremism, as well as courageous public officials.
   c. the passage of the Nineteenth Amendment.
   d. the work of evangelist Billy Sunday.

9. The National Origins Quota Act of 1924 was
   a. a reaction to increasing Nordic immigrants.
   b. a response by some to a general rise in rates of immigration.
   c. an attempt by some to establish racial purity as an immigration policy.
   d. an effort to increase immigration from southeastern Europe.

10. The Scopes trial indicated that
    a. traditional rural religious beliefs were stronger than ever.
    b. fundamentalism died with the victory of Clarence Darrow.
    c. Darwin's theory was proved wrong.
    d. none of the above

11. The Democratic Party in the 1920s
    a. won only one presidential election.
    b. gained many new voters among the cities' ethnic groups.
    c. gained converts in rural areas.

12. During his presidency, Warren G. Harding
    a. allowed some friends to abuse their power.
    b. exposed and tried to clean up the Teapot Dome scandal.
    c. was deeply involved in corruption and bribes.
    d. was not well liked, but was an effective president.

13. As president, Calvin Coolidge
    a. was friendly to American business interests.
    b. was as corrupt as Harding.
    c. worked hard and long at being a good president.
    d. ran for another term as president and barely won.

14. Republican policies of the 1920s favored
    a. low tariffs, low taxes, and cuts in government spending.
    b. high tariffs, low taxes, and cuts in government spending.
    c. high tariffs, high taxes, and cuts in government spending.
    d. low tariffs, high taxes, and increases in government spending.

15. In the 1920s, American agricultural lobbies succeeded in
    a. solving the problems of overproduction.
    b. dumping surpluses overseas at a low price.
    c. passing higher tariffs for some crops.
    d. overcoming a serious wartime recession.

THOUGHT QUESTIONS

To check your understanding of the key issues of this period, solve the following problems:

1. How was the economic revolution of the 1920s different from the changes of the latter part of the nineteenth century?

2. List the elements of American life that were changed by the automobile.

3. What groups did not share in the prosperity of the 1920s?

4. Compare the women's movement of the 1920s with other similar movements in American history.

5. Speculate on why the literary movement of the 1920s was so critical of contemporary American life.

6. Herbert Hoover called prohibition a "noble experiment." What were the results of that experiment?

7. Summarize the policies of the Republican presidents of the 1920s. What were the results of these policies?

CHAPTER 26

FRANKLIN D. ROOSEVELT AND THE NEW DEAL

SUMMARY
After a great rise in the stock market, the 1929 crash brought about an economic depression, which had to be dealt with by Hoover, and then, more successfully, by Franklin Delano Roosevelt.

THE GREAT DEPRESSION
The economy of the United States collapsed after 1929, creating the single worst panic and era of unemployment in the nation's history.

The Great Bull Market
From 1927 to 1929, the stock market experienced a sharp increase known as the great bull market, caused by easy credit, inflated currency, and margin loans. This bubble burst in the fall of 1929 in the stock market crash.

Effect of the Depression
This was the start of a decade of terrible economic conditions. Eventually, the Great Depression became the worst downturn in the nation's history.

FIGHTING THE DEPRESSION
Ending the depression became the most important political issue of the 1930s, as first a Republican president and then a Democrat tried to achieve economic recovery.

Hoover and Voluntarism
Hoover emphasized voluntary solutions to the economic ills of the nation, using government only minimally. But his efforts failed to stop the deteriorating health of business.

The Emergence of Roosevelt
In 1932 the voters overwhelmingly elected Franklin D. Roosevelt to the presidency.

The Hundred Days
With a clear understanding of the responsibilities of political leadership, Roosevelt asserted his authority with the banking crisis. After this success, he proceeded to pass several significant reforms in the first three months of his initial term.

Roosevelt and Relief
He pushed through Congress several acts which attempted to provide immediate help to the hungry and homeless.

ROOSEVELT AND REFORM
After pressure developed for more fundamental reform, Roosevelt responded by suggesting permanent changes in the economic arrangements and institutions of the United States.

Angry Voices
Several critics complained about the New Deal and the still ailing economy, suggesting more radical reforms were in order.

Social Security
Roosevelt secured passage of the Social Security Act, which provided only modest pensions and unemployment insurance.

Labor Legislation
The president also supported legislation which guaranteed the rights of workers to organize and bargain collectively, then endorsed a law which provided for maximum hours and a minimum wage.

IMPACT OF THE NEW DEAL
Roosevelt's program, known as the New Deal, succeeded in improving some, if not all, elements of American society.

Rise of Organized Labor
The New Deal resulted in a dramatic increase in union membership, especially among the unskilled.

The New Deal Record on Help to Minorities
However, with only a few exceptions, the New Deal did not address the problems of the nation's minorities.

Women at Work
For most women the Depression caused a worsening of their position in the economy.

END OF THE NEW DEAL
After five years of significant success, Roosevelt could no longer secure passage of new reforms and his New Deal came to an end.

The Election of 1936
Roosevelt and his party won a landslide victory in the elections of 1936 but
several factors combined to close the New Deal.

The Supreme Court Fight
Roosevelt's effort to reorganize the Supreme Court failed in Congress; a significant coalition that opposed the president resulted.

The New Deal in Decline
The recession of 1937 and the unsuccessful "Purge of '38" revived the Republican party and strengthened opposition to Roosevelt's programs in Congress.

Evaluation of the New Deal
The New Deal did not cure the problems of the Depression, nor did it radicalize the nation's economy, but it did have a positive psychological impact on the public, made some permanent reforms, and left the Democratic party as the majority party for decades.

LEARNING OBJECTIVES

After mastering this chapter, you should be able to

1. Explain the causes of the "great bull market."

2. Describe the effects of the great depression.

3. Discuss President Hoover's attempts to end the Depression.

4. Analyze the New Deal legislation passed in the "Hundred Days."

5. Differentiate between Roosevelt's programs for relief and recovery.

6. List and evaluate New Deal reforms.

7. Compare and contrast the programs of the various critics of the New Deal.

8. Show how the New Deal affected labor, women, and minorities.

9. Narrate the events and explain the significance of Roosevelt's attempt to "pack the court."

10. Discuss the factors that ended the New Deal.

GLOSSARY

To build your social science vocabulary, familiarize yourself with the following terms:

1. **speculative** pertaining to buying stocks or goods at risk, hoping for great gains in the future. "Investors who had borrowed heavily to take part in the speculative mania which swept Wall Street. . . ."

2. **deprivation** the state of being deprived or dispossessed. "Children grew up thinking that economic deprivation was the norm. . . ."

3. **durable goods** long-lasting goods, typically automobiles and appliances. ". . . a natural consequence as more and more people already owned these durable goods."

4. **margin** in the stock market, the amount of the broker's loan to an investor to encourage the purchase of stock. "Corporations used their large cash reserves to supply money to brokers who in turn loaned it to investors on margin. . . ."

5. **stoop labor** a type of hard farm labor in which the worker must bend over at the waist for long hours. ". . . angry citizens, now willing to do stoop labor in the fields. . . ."

6. **vagrants** those who have no home. ". . . the number of vagrants increased. . . ."

7. **nuances** small gradations in meaning or significance. " . . . he had little patience with philosophical nuances. . . ."

8. **solvent** able to pay all debts. "Other banks, once they became solvent, would open later. . . ."

9. **allocate** to assign or distribute for a particular purpose. " . . . allocate acreage among individual farmers. . . ."

10. **collective bargaining** the process of negotiating the terms of work between management and a union representing all the workers. ". . . the guarantee of collective bargaining. . . ."

11. **morass** something sticky or impeding. "The NRA quickly bogged down in a huge bureaucratic morass."

12. **allotments** assigned, designated, or distributed portions. "The system of allotments. . . ."

13. **dole** charity; money given to the poor by government. " . . . helping those who had been unemployed for years to get off the dole. . . ."

14. **anti-Semitism** prejudice, discrimination, or hostility against Jews. ". . . Coughlin appealed to the discontented with a strange mixture of crank monetary schemes and anti-Semitism."

15. **regressive** (regarding taxation) any system that lays the heaviest burden on the poor. "The regressive feature of the act was even worse."

IDENTIFICATION

Briefly identify the meaning and significance of the following terms.

1. Reconstruction Finance Corporation (RFC) _____

2. National Recovery Administration (NRA) _____

3. Agricultural Adjustment Act (AAA) _____

4. Harry Hopkins _____

5. Works Progress Administration (WPA) _____

6. Townsend Plan _____

7. Social Security Act _____

8. Wagner Act _____

9. John L. Lewis _____

_____

10. Liberty League _____

_____

MATCHING

A. Match the following legislative acts or government agencies to the appropriate description.

____1. Federal Farm Board   a. established minimum wages and maximum hours for some workers

____2. Farm Security Administration   b. developed programs for school-age Americans

____3. Civilian Conservation Corps   c. purchased surplus commodities and loaned money to cooperatives

____4. National Youth Administration   d. loaned money to financial institutions to save them from bankruptcy

____5. Fair Labor Standards Act   e. helped tenants and sharecroppers acquire land

     f. employed city youths to work in the country on public parks and recreational sites

B. Match the following individuals with the appropriate description.

____1. Charles Coughlin   a. nominee of the Union party for president in 1936

____2. Francis Townsend   b. secretary of labor and first woman cabinet member

____3. Huey Long   c. energetic leader of New Deal relief

____4. William Lemke   d. Detroit Roman Catholic radio commentator who became a critic of the New Deal

_____ 5. Frances Perkins
                                       e. colorful senator from Louisiana who started the "share the wealth" movement

                                       f. doctor who proposed a pension for the elderly

COMPLETION

Answer the question or complete the statement by filling in the blanks with the correct word or words.

1. One of President Hoover's public-works projects was the building of _____.

2. World War I veterans were forced out of the shacks in Washington, D.C., by _____.

3. Section 7a of the New Deal's industrial recovery legislation protected the rights of _____.

4. The blue eagle was a symbol of cooperation with the _____.

5. Roosevelt's secretary of agriculture was _____.

6. The National Union for Social Justice was the idea of _____.

7. The legislation that guaranteed unions the rights of collective bargaining was the _____.

8. Electricity was provided to 90 percent of America's farms by the _____.

9. John L. Lewis's group, which was expelled from the American Federation of Labor, became known as the _____.

10. The leader in the Senate opposition to the court-packing plan was Montana's _____.

TRUE/FALSE

Mark the following statements either T (True) or F (False).

_____ 1. Public policy of the 1920s tried to discourage speculative investment.

_____ 2. President Hoover did nothing to try to solve the problems of the Depression.

_____3. President Roosevelt succeeded in preserving private ownership of the nation's banks.

_____4. The Agricultural Adjustment Act allowed the government to set production quotas for certain crops.

_____5. President Roosevelt spent too much money in trying to provide relief from the Depression.

_____6. The New Deal reform legislation tried to correct all of the nation's social and economic injustices.

_____7. The greatest successes of the New Deal were the attempts to aid minorities.

_____8. The Indian Reorganization Act of 1934 stressed tribal unity.

_____9. On balance, the 1930s was a dismal decade for American women.

_____10. The economic successes of 1937 indicated that the New Deal had cured the Depression.

MULTIPLE CHOICE

Circle the one alternative that *best* completes the statement or answers the question.

1. One of the reasons for the "great bull market" was that
   a. a majority of Americans bought and sold stock.
   b. the productivity of the American economy was well distributed among the population.
   c. investors could get easy credit for broker's loans.
   d. the Federal Reserve Board raised the discount rate.

2. Herbert Hoover's solution to the Depression was to
   a. provide some federal help to farmers, but leave relief to the poor private and voluntary.
   b. provide no help at all.
   c. help all levels of the economy, but in an amount consistent with a balanced budget.
   d. lower tariffs and thus increase foreign trade.

3. The purpose of the Agricultural Adjustment Act was to
   a. ensure that no one starved.
   b. raise farm income by restricting production.
   c. socialize America's farms.
   d. protect the rights of farm tenants and sharecroppers.

4. The significance of the Works Progress Administration was that it
   a. funded a variety of projects, including theater, writing, and art, as well as buildings and parks.
   b. was the idea of Huey Long.
   c. established the rights of unions to organize and bargain collectively.
   d. became a permanent federal agency.

5. Father Charles Coughlin attacked the New Deal, suggesting that
   a. everyone over sixty should receive $200 per month.
   b. money should be inflated and the banks nationalized.
   c. there should be a "share the wealth" program.
   d. the nation should encourage Jewish immigration from Germany.

6. The Social Security Act provided for all of the following *except*
   a. old-age pensions.
   b. unemployment compensation.
   c. welfare grants.
   d. aid to the nation's migrants.

7. During the New Deal, organized labor
   a. received support from the government, but declined in membership.
   b. received support from government and gained membership.
   c. won most of its major goals with no violent strikes.
   d. took a united and aggressive approach to organizing the unskilled.

8. The New Deal handled past inequities to minorities by
   a. passing civil rights legislation.
   b. making sure that all programs were "color-blind."
   c. confronting squarely the racial injustice in federal relief programs.
   d. none of the above

9. The Roosevelt coalition included
   a. farmers, small-town whites, and big business.
   b. native-stock Americans, the wealthy, and big-city machines.
   c. urban, ethnic, labor, and African American voters
   d. the rural Northeast, the solid South, and the small towns of the Midwest.

10. Which of the following is an accurate evaluation of the New Deal?
    a. It was clearly socialist in intent and impact.
    b. It was moderate and relatively ineffective economically, but did produce sweeping political changes, putting the Democratic party in the majority.
    c. It was a successful revolution that achieved the goal of equal opportunity and social justice.
    d. It achieved little except for equality for women and minorities.

11. Which of the following was *not* a cause of the Great Depression?
    a. More goods were produced than consumers could use.
    b. There were unstable economic conditions in Europe.
    c. Many U.S. corporations were mismanaged.
    d. High taxes for the social security system took too high a percentage of the federal budget.

12. The National Recovery Administration tried to guarantee
    a. minority rights.
    b. freedom from unions.
    c. codes of fair practice.
    d. no government interferences.

13. The problem solved by the New Deal farm policy that had previously been ignored was
    a. monopoly in the farm-implements business.
    b. irrigation.
    c. crop rotation.
    d. overproduction.

14. The Great Depression
    a. caused most Americans to favor radical politics.
    b. was expected and many Americans had planned for it.
    c. caused many to doubt America's strength and future.
    d. affected the upper and lower classes, but left the middle class largely untouched.

15. The effect of the "court-packing" scheme was to
    a. end the power of the Supreme Court.
    b. increase the number of judges on the court to fifteen.
    c. weaken the president's relations with Congress.
    d. jeopardize Roosevelt's popularity with older Americans.

THOUGHT QUESTIONS

To check your understanding of the key issues of this period, solve the following problems:

1. Compare and contrast the first and second New Deals. Comment on possible explanations for the different approaches.

2. "The differences between Hoover and Roosevelt were more appearance than reality." Comment. To what extent is this true, and in what ways is it false?

3. What were the permanent changes of the New Deal? Were these changes for the better or not?

4. Compare the New Deal with other reform movements, such as populism and progressivism.

5. Comment on the extent to which Roosevelt's personality affected the course of the New Deal.

6. What set of factors ended Roosevelt's legislative successes? What could he have done to preserve and extend his influence?

CHAPTER 27

AMERICA AND THE WORLD, 1921-1945

SUMMARY
After remaining primarily isolationist through the 1930s, the United States became increasingly involved in world affairs and took a leading role in maintaining world order.

RETREAT, REVERSAL, AND RIVALRY
In the 1920s, the United States followed a foreign policy that was narrow, cautious, and self-centered.

Retreat in Europe
Regarding Europe, American policymakers insisted on payment of war debts without allowing access to American markets and, thus, the dollars necessary to pay those debts.

Cooperation in Latin America
In Latin America, the United States continued to seek economic advantages, but did so with more friendly tactics than had previous administrations.

Rivalry in Asia
In Asia, the United States continued on a confrontational course with Japan.

ISOLATIONISM
Because of the Great Depression and the threat of European war, the United States followed an isolationist policy in the 1930s.

The Lure of Pacifism and Neutrality
Looking back at World War I as a meaningless effort, many Americans sought security in pacifism and legal neutrality. They wanted a way to ensure that the United States would not be drawn into a European conflict.

War in Europe
Events in in Europe made this posture increasingly unrealistic and difficult to maintain, and the neutrality acts became became harder to support.

THE ROAD TO WAR
From 1939 to 1941, the United States moved ever closer to war as the nation's sympathy and support went to England and France.

From Neutrality to Undeclared War
As the war worsened in Europe, President Roosevelt pushed the country closer to participation. He clearly favored the Allied cause and convinced Congress to relax the strict neutrality acts in order to aid the British.

Showdown in the Pacific
A surprise attack by the Japanese on Pearl Harbor plunged the nation into war.

TURNING THE TIDE AGAINST THE AXIS
In both Europe and Asia the early days of the war were discouraging for Americans, although several factors developed that allowed the Allies to halt the advance of the Axis powers.

Wartime Partnerships
Most importantly, the alliance of the United States and Britain was a genuine coalition with unified command and strategy, while the Soviet Union took the worst fury of the German *blitzkrieg*.

Halting the German *Blitz*
The United States and Britain invaded first North Africa and then Italy, while the Soviet Union stopped the Germans at Stalingrad.

Checking Japan in the Pacific
In Asia, the United States navy gained control of the Central Pacific by July of 1942.

THE HOME FRONT
The war wrought vast changes in American society and ended the decade of depression.

A Nation on the Move
The war motivated millions to migrate, creating problems in housing and family life, but offering opportunities to African Americans and women. Another important problem was the relocation of Japanese Americans into concentration camps.

Win-the-War Politics
Politically, Roosevelt and the Democrats maintained power and won wartime elections.

VICTORY
After the offensives of the Axis powers had been stopped, the war ended quickly. The Germans were thoroughly defeated and forced to surrender unconditionally.

War Aims and Wartime Diplomacy
The alliance between the United States and the Soviet Union ended. The two countries had far different goals concerning the rebuilding of postwar Europe.

Triumph and Tragedy in the Pacific
Though the war in Europe was over, the war in the Pacific continued until President Harry S. Truman ordered the dropping of two atomic bombs on Japan.

LEARNING OBJECTIVES

After mastering this chapter, you should be able to

1. Summarize the foreign policy of the United States in the 1920s.

2. Explain the causes and effects of the isolationism of the 1930s.

3. Trace the background of war in Europe in the 1930s.

4. Discuss the factors that led to conflict in Asia.

5. Analyze the goals of the Allies in forming the wartime coalition.

6. Discuss the military strategy which stopped the advance of the Germans.

7. Describe how the United States took control of the Central Pacific in 1942.

8. Discuss the changes the war brought about in domestic economic development.

9. Describe the impact of the war on minorities, women, and labor unions.

10. Explain the impact of war on American politics.

11. Evaluate the performance of the United States in wartime diplomacy.

12. Discuss the Allied strategy of the last days of World War II.

GLOSSARY

To build your social science vocabulary, familiarize yourself with the following terms:

1. **pacifists** those who oppose war or the unrestricted use of the military. ". . . especially among pacifists who had advocated the outlawing of war. . . ."

2. **bilateral** in diplomacy, pertaining to an action or treaty involving two nations. "An unhappy Briand, who had wanted a bilateral treaty with the United States. . . ."

3. **reparations** payment or indemnification for loss after a war. ". . . they were forced to scale down their demands for German reparations. . . ."

4. **repudiate** discard; disavow; reject. ". . . the ungrateful Allies were trying to repudiate their sacred obligations."

5. **estrangement** the act of alienating or avoiding friendly relations. ". . . Roosevelt finally ended the long estrangement. . . ."

6. **subversive** tending to ruin, destroy, or overthrow. "The Soviets soon went back on promises to stop all subversive activity. . . ."

7. **charismatic** having a magnetic personality or attraction. "A shrewd and charismatic leader . . ."

8. **Reich** German word for rule, kingdom, or reign. ". . . uniting all Germans into a Greater Third Reich. . . ."

9. **belligerents** nations engaged in war. ". . . ban arms sales and loans to belligerents. . . ."

10. **coup** a sudden and decisive forcible change in the government of a nation. ". . . he seized Austria in a bloodless coup."

11. **Anglophiles** those who favor or have an affinity for the people and institutions of Britain. "Eastern Anglophiles, moderate New Dealers, and liberal Republicans made up the bulk of the membership. . . ."

12. **depreciation** (in taxation) a tax break based on the fact that machinery wears out or loses value. "The WPB allowed business rapid depreciation, and thus huge tax credits. . . ."

13. **detention** restraint or confinement. "Herded into hastily built detention centers. . . ."

14. **Balkan** an area of south central Europe, a peninsula bounded by the Aegean and Adriatic seas. "As his armies overran Poland and the Balkan countries. . . ."

15. **capitulation** a surrender with stated conditions. ". . . Japan signed a formal capitulation agreement. . . ."

IDENTIFICATION

Briefly identify the meaning and significance of the following terms.

1. Kellogg-Briand Treaty

2. Washington Conference

3. Adolf Hitler

4. Nye Committee

5. America First Committee

6. War Production Board

7. Fair Employment Practices Committee

8. "zoot suit" riots

9. D-Day

10. Manhattan Project

MATCHING

A. Match the following world leaders with the appropriate description.

_____ 1. Haile Selassie   **a.** dictator of Italy before and during World War II

_____ 2. Chiang Kai-shek   **b.** emperor of Ethiopia during the Italian invasion

_____ 3. Hideki Tojo   **c.** leader of the Soviet Union during World War II

_____ 4. Charles de Gaulle   **d.** leader of the Nationalist Chinese during World War II

_____ 5. Joseph Stalin   **e.** Japanese army militant who became premier in 1941

     f. leader of exile government known as the Free French

B. Match the following leaders with the appropriate description.

_____ 1. Cordell Hull   **a.** head of the Committee to Defend America by Aiding the Allies

_____ 2. Gerald Nye   **b.** aviator-hero and member of the America First Committee

_____ 3. William Allen White   **c.** secretary of state under President Franklin D. Roosevelt

_____ 4. Donald Nelson   **d.** African American labor leader who demanded equal employment opportunities during World War II

_____ 5. A. Philip Randolph   **e.** Sears, Roebuck executive and head of the War Production Board

     f. senator who sponsored the neutrality acts of 1935, 1936, and 1937

COMPLETION

Answer the question or complete the statement by filling in the blanks with the correct word or words.

1. The 1928 treaty intended to outlaw war was the _____.

2. The Roosevelt Corollary to the Monroe Doctrine was repudiated by the _____.

3. A 1921 attempt to achieve naval disarmament was called the _____.

4. To avoid a two-front war, Hitler signed the _____ with Russia.

5. The Republicans nominated ex-Democrat _____ to run against President Roosevelt in 1940.

6. The German Afrika Korps was led by _____.

7. The American leader of the naval attack on key Japanese islands in the Pacific was _____.

8. President Roosevelt dropped his liberal Vice President Henry Wallace in 1944 and chose the moderate _____.

9. A developing split between the Soviet Union and the United States became apparent at the July 1945 meeting at _____.

10. A commitee headed by _____ suggested dropping an atomic bomb on a Japanese city.

TRUE/FALSE

Mark the following statements either T (True) or F (False).

_____1. United States tariff policy of the 1920s welcomed European products and thus helped the Allies pay their war debts.

_____2. The United States remained aloof from the problems of Europe between the wars.

_____3. The United States achieved some foreign-policy successes in Latin America between the wars.

_____4. Economic depression and the threat of war made the United States more isolationist in the 1930s.

_____5. Americans were eager to oppose the rise of fascism in Europe in the 1930s.

_____6. American neutrality was inconsequential in the affairs of Europe in the 1920s.

_____7. President Roosevelt believed that a German victory threatened American security.

_____8. Because of Pearl Harbor, the United States decided to defeat the Japanese first before attacking Germany.

_____9. The Soviet Union suffered more losses of life and property than did the other Allies fighting the Nazi threat.

_____10. President Truman considered for several months the decision to drop the atomic bomb.

MULTIPLE CHOICE

Circle the one alternative that *best* completes the statement or answers the question.

1. After World War I the United States
   a. lowered tariffs to encourage trade.
   b. was the richest nation on earth.
   c. canceled its allies' war debts.
   d. aggressively sought collective security.

2. Regarding Latin America, President Roosevelt
   a. succeeded in improving relations and renounced the imperialism of the past.
   b. followed a combination of the "big stick" and "dollar diplomacy."
   c. sent marines into several nations.
   d. reestablished the "Roosevelt Corollary."

3. The treaties of the Washington Conference
   a. reduced the level of all naval construction.
   b. was one of the important accomplishments of the League of Nations.
   c. closed the "Open Door" in China.
   d. failed to maintain the status quo in the Pacific.

4. The United States followed an isolationist policy in the 1930s because
   a. World War I had made the world safe for democracy.
   b. our European allies had defaulted on the American loans.
   c. of the Depression and the threat of war.
   d. of opposition to the rise of Hitler.

5. In the 1930s, Japan, Germany, and Italy were
   a. strongly anticommunist.
   b. no threat to their neighbors.
   c. supporters of the League of Nations.
   d. satisfied with the world status quo.

6. Which of the following was not an element of the pacifist movement of the 1930s?
   a. the novel *All Quiet on the Western Front*
   b. the efforts of rich families such as the Krupps and the DuPonts
   c. American youth on college campuses
   d. the "merchants-of-death" thesis

7. The neutrality acts
   a. tried to insulate the United States from European problems.
   b. had no impact on European affairs.
   c. received the strong support of President Roosevelt.
   d. limited the war to Europe and Asia.

8. Increasing defense expenditures, the peacetime draft, and lend-lease indicated that Americans
   a. wanted to declare war on Germany.
   b. feared the results of German victory.
   c. wanted to respond to Pearl Harbor.
   d. desired to dominate Latin America.

9. The effect of the attack on Pearl Harbor was to
   a. divide the country politically on foreign policy.
   b. bring about war with Japan but not Germany.
   c. shock Americans into an awareness of the Axis threat.
   d. all of the above.

10. The wartime Allied coalition was
    a. especially close and effective between the United States and Britain.
    b. based on American and Free French cooperation.
    c. no more effective than the Berlin-Rome-Tokyo Axis.
    d. difficult because the United States had not recognized the Soviet Union.

11. At the meeting of the Western Allies at Casablanca it was decided that
    a. the war in Europe was successful enough to avoid a beachhead assault.
    b. use of the atomic bomb would be restricted to Asia.
    c. Russia would create a "second front" with Germany.
    d. they would fight the Axis powers until they achieved an unconditional surrender.

12. Americans who stayed at home during World War II
    a. had to make major adjustments in their lives.
    b. found that society changed little.
    c. seldom moved.
    d. could at least enjoy the abundance of consumer goods.

13. Which of the following was not a U.S. problem of the war years?
    a. a housing shortage
    b. racial problems in integrated combat units
    c. racial discrimination in industry
    d. an increased divorce rate

14. Japanese-Americans were
    a. treated as badly as Germany treated Jews.
    b. often denied their liberty and their property.
    c. allowed to fight but only in the Pacific.
    d. treated differently depending on whether they were first- or second-generation immigrants.

15. The 1944 Republican presidential nominee, Thomas E. Dewey,
    a. ran as a peace candidate.
    b. ran as an opponent of the New Deal.
    c. focused on the issue of international organization.
    d. argued that Roosevelt's health was poor and that Democrats were "soft on communism."

THOUGHT QUESTIONS

To check your understanding of the key issues of this period, solve the following problems:

1. To what extent did the American retreat from responsibility in foreign affairs aid the rise of dictators in the 1930s?

2. Comment on the allegation that in the 1920s and 1930s there was no change in the U.S.-Latin American policy goals; that is, economic dominance of the Western Hemisphere. Was the "Good Neighbor" policy merely a change in tactics?

3. Considering the reasons for conflict in Asia, how surprising was the attack on Pearl Harbor?

4. What were the long-range effects of World War II on American society?

5. What was the role of historical interpretation in the foreign policy of the 1930s, specifically the neutrality acts?

6. What were the various goals of the Allied powers? How did these different goals affect the coalition, the strategy, and the outcome of the war?

7. Do you think that President Roosevelt "sold us out" at the Yalta Conference? What was the Soviet perspective on Eastern Europe?

CHAPTER 28

TRUMAN AND THE COLD WAR

SUMMARY
Postwar antagonism gradually led the United States and the Soviet Union into the Cold War. The contrasts between the countries were dramatically represented in their leaders-Truman who believed in the innate goodness of America; Stalin the hard-headed realist who was determined to protect Russia's wartime conquests.

THE COLD WAR BEGINS
The two countries split over three issues: control of Europe, economic aid, and the control of atomic weapons.

The Division of Europe
The Allies first divided over the division of Europe, with each side insisting on imposing its values in the areas liberated by its military. The division of Germany between West (where the U.S., Britain and France exercised authority) and East (under the Soviets) was most crucial.

Withholding Economic Aid
They also disagreed over the terms of assistance needed for the economic reconstruction of Russia, leading the U.S. to end Lend-Lease and to ignore a Soviet request for a loan.

The Atomic Dilemma
Most important, the United States proposed a very gradual abolition of nuclear arms, while the Soviets proposed immediate nuclear disarmament. Any attempt to agree on mutual reduction of atomic weapons failed.

CONTAINMENT
America's foreign policy leaders, Marshall, Acheson, and Kennan, initiated a major departure in American foreign affairs by proposing a policy of "containment" of the USSR.

The Truman Doctrine
In 1947, President Truman asked Congress for money for aid to Greece and Turkey, thereby assuming what had been Great Britain's role, that of the leading power in the eastern Mediterranean. "Cold War" was then declared against the Russians.

The Marshall Plan
The American government also decided to contain Soviet influence by financing postwar European recovery as a check on communist power. The plan paid rich dividends by helping the industrial revival in western Europe and ending the threat of a communist dominated continent.

The Western Military Alliance
With the establishment of the NATO western military alliance, the United States overreacted to Soviet aggression. Tensions between the former allies escalated.

The Berlin Blockade
Finally, when the Russians blockaded the western access to Berlin, the Truman government responded with an airlift which maintained the American position in that German city. The Cold War had cut Europe in two.

THE COLD WAR EXPANDS
In the late 1940s and the early 1950s, the Cold War expanded. Both sides built up their military might, and diplomatic competition spread from Europe to Asia.

The Military Dimension
Committed to winning the growing conflict with Russia, the American government unified its armed services and initiated a massive military buildup, especially of its air force. The National Security Act created the CIA and the president's National Security Council.

The Cold War in Asia
In Asia, the United States consolidated its Pacific sphere, and then failed to avert the Chinese civil war in which Mao Tse-tung and the Communists drove Chiang Kai-shek from the mainland to Formosa (renamed Taiwan).

The Korean War
The Cold War Asian showdown came in Korea, where the North Koreans invaded the South-perhaps without Soviet approval-leading to a war in which the United States defended its original containment objective at the 38th parallel. The most significant result of the war might have been the massive rearming of America.

THE COLD WAR AT HOME
President Truman tried, for the most part unsuccessfully, to revive the New Deal reform tradition after World War II.

Truman's Troubles
Truman's apparent lack of vision and his fondness for appointing friends and cronies to high office were major weaknesses. Also, the postwar mood of the country was not conducive to further reform efforts. Truman found himself in the middle, caught, for example, between union demands for higher wages and the public demand that prices be kept down.

Truman Vindicated

The president benefitted from Thomas Dewey's passive campaign and the indecisiveness of the Republican-led Congress and won the 1948 presidential election. Reminding the voters of the past successes of the New Deal and of his aggressiveness in the Cold War, Truman confounded the pollsters by winning a decisive victory.

The Loyalty Issue

Fear of communists and subversives led to a government-initiated loyalty program and unrelenting investigations by the House Un-American Activities Committee. Alger Hiss was convicted of perjury after allegations of espionage were presented by Whittaker Chambers. Thousands of government workers were dismissed by the Loyalty Review Board for dubious loyalty. Soviet detonation of an A-bomb in 1949 led to the conviction and execution of Julius and Ethel Rosenberg for conspiring with the Soviets.

McCarthyism in Action

Heightened American fear of communism prompted Senator Joseph McCarthy into a tireless pursuit of communist conspirators. McCarthy directed his accusations toward practically any target, from the State Department to the army. Among those he accused of communist sympathies were Secretary of State Dean Acheson and General George Marshall.

The Republicans in Power

Promising to "clean up the mess in Washington" and to bring the Korean War to an honorable end, Dwight Eisenhower won the election for the Republicans in 1952. Eisenhower succeeded in reaching agreement with the North Koreans for an armistice in 1953. With regard to McCarthy's allegations at home, the president played for time. In the end, McCarthy's unfounded accusations led to public humiliation and censure before the Senate in 1954. His influence was such that cultural conformity was demanded, and political dissent was frozen until the end of the decade.

LEARNING OBJECTIVES

After mastering this chapter, you should be able to

1. Describe the Soviet purposes in establishing pro-Russian regimes in eastern Europe, then describe and evaluate the American response.

2. Specify the condition of the Soviet economy at the end of World War II, then describe and evaluate the American response to the Russian request for a loan.

3. Identify and describe the three men who led in the development of the containment policy; then define the policy and explain its significance in the Cold War.

4. Identify the Marshall Plan and explain and evaluate the American purposes in implementing the program.

5. Describe, explain, and evaluate the American establishment of the NATO military alliance.

6. Examine the Berlin blockade crisis and its resolution.

7. Discuss the origins and development of the Korean War and the United States confusion about its objectives.

8. Relate how McCarthy played to the fears of his fellow citizens and how he overstepped the bounds of integrity.

9. Compare and contrast the Soviet and American postwar proposals for dealing with atomic weapons.

10. Analyze the perception of crisis that led to the development of the containment policy first presented with the Truman Doctrine.

11. Describe the American military mobilization of 1947-1950.

12. Delineate the American and Russian postwar spheres of influence in Asia, then trace the U.S. consolidation and defense of its sphere.

13. Evaluate Truman's weaknesses as president and yet his success in winning the election in 1948.

14. Account for America's extreme reaction to the postwar "Red Scare."

15. Identify how Eisenhower was able to take advantage of the Cold War crisis and domestic disturbance to achieve consensus and popularity.

GLOSSARY

To build your social science vocabulary, familiarize yourself with the following terms:

1. **reparations** payments by a defeated nation to victors for war damages and losses. ". . . Truman and Stalin clashed . . . over such difficult issues as reparations. . . ."

2. **coalition** union or alliance, often temporary, among factions, parties, or nations. ". . . Communist regimes replaced coalition governments. . . ."

3. **coup** a successful decisive action, especially the overthrow of a government. ". . . a coup in Czechoslovakia . . . gave the Soviets a strategic foothold in central Europe."

4. **strategic** pertaining to the planning and directing of large-scale forces to achieve security or victory. "... a coup in Czechoslovakia ... gave the Soviets a strategic foothold in Central Europe."

5. **demobilization** disbandment, especially of military forces. "... Eisenhower ... cited the rapid demobilization of American armed forces...."

6. **appeasement** bringing peace, especially when done with conciliatory concessions. "Recalling the lesson of Munich, he opposed appeasement...."

7. **trusteeship** control of the administration of a territory, usually by appointment of an international organization. "A trusteeship arrangement ... merely disguised the fact that the United States held full control over the ... islands."

8. **mediation** the attempt to resolve differences through an intermediary. "Political mediation had failed, military intervention was out of the question."

9. **collective security** pertaining to the organization of a group of nations to guarantee the security of each member nation. "... the President ... secured a resolution ... calling on the member nations to engage in a collective-security action."

10. **satellite** a country dominated by a more powerful nation. "... the United States was at war with a Soviet satellite in Asia."

11. **tactical** pertaining to maneuvers for gaining an advantage over an adversary. "...he waited ... ready to dazzle an opponent with ... tactical mastery."

12. **intelligence** secret information, usually about an adversary. "... the act created the Central Intelligence Agency (CIA) to coordinate the intelligence-gathering activities...."

13. **legitimacy** a state of lawfulness according to accepted standards. "... the state department refused to recognize the legitimacy of the new regime in Peking...."

14. **truce** a temporary end to fighting by agreement of the belligerents. "... as truce talks with the Communists bogged down...."

15. **bipartisan** involving cooperation or agreement between two parties (usually, in American history, Republicans and Democrats). "The Republicans, committed to support the bipartisan policy of containment...."

IDENTIFICATION

Briefly identify the meaning and significance of the following terms.

1. containment _____

_____

2. Truman Doctrine _____

_____

3. Marshall Plan _____

_____

4. NATO _____

_____

5. Berlin blockade _____

_____

6. Chinese civil war _____

_____

7. Korean War _____

_____

8. Taft-Hartley Act of 1947 _____

_____

9. Alger Hiss trial _____

_____

10. McCarthyism _____

_____

MATCHING

A. Match the following leaders with the appropriate description.

____1. Bernard Baruch

____2. George C. Marshall

____3. Dean Acheson

____4. George Kennan

____5. Arthur M. Vandenberg

a. head of Policy Planning Staff who drafted NSC-68 as a statement of defense policy

b. senator who suggested that Truman scare Americans to get their backing for containment

c. secretary of state who helped redirect American policy toward containment

d. undersecretary of state who hoped to see the United States take Britain's role as a leading great power

e. financier who drafted a plan that preserved America's monopoly of the atomic bomb

f. head of Policy Planning Staff who first advocated containment of Soviet power

B. Match the following Cold War figures with the appropriate description.

____1. Andrei Gromyko

____2. Mao Tse-tung

____3. Kim Il-Sung

____4. Alger Hiss

____5. Strom Thurmond

a. Chinese Communist leader who won control of the Chinese mainland

b. North Korean who launched attack on South Korea in 1950

c. State Department official accused of being a communist spy—convicted of perjury

d. leader of the Dixiecrats in the 1948 presidential campaign

e. Russian diplomat who proposed a total ban on atomic bombs

f. Soviet leader who intensified the Cold War after Russia's success with Sputnik

COMPLETION

Answer the question or complete the statement by filling in the blanks with the correct word or words.

1. The earliest Soviet-American conflicts concerned occupation and reparations in _____.

2. The Truman Doctrine resulted when the United States took over the British role in the eastern Mediterranean by providing aid for _____ and _____.

3. The two possible forms of postwar assistance to shattered Europe were _____ and _____.

4. The nationalist forces in the Chinese civil war were led by _____.

5. After securing a resolution condemning North Korea as an aggressor, the U.N. Security Council called on member nations to engage in a _____ action.

6. McCarthy's basic technique in leveling charges of treasonable activities was the _____.

7. The congressional committee that investigated alleged subversives and communists after the war was the _____.

8. The repentant communist who accused Alger Hiss of passing classified State Department documents was _____.

9. The Democratic party splinter group that bolted from the party in 1948 and nominated Strom Thurmond for the presidency was known as the _____.

10. The congressional act that overrode President Truman's veto and was designed to correct the imbalance in labor-management relations was the _____.

TRUE/FALSE

Mark the following statements either T (True) or F (False).

_____1. When compared to the blunt and belligerent Stalin, Harry Truman seemed cautious and cunning.

_____2. The Russians refused to participate in the Marshall Plan because they saw it as an attempt to weaken their control of eastern Europe.

_____3. NSC-68 argued that the United States could afford to spend no more than thirty percent of its gross national product for military security.

_____4. As the spheres of influence were defined at Yalta, China fell between the American and Russian spheres.

_____5. Secretary of State Dean Acheson argued that the civil war in China was beyond the control of the government of the United States.

_____6. Secretary Acheson and General MacArthur warned President Truman of the dangers of Chinese entrance into the Korean War.

_____7. The most important issue in the 1948 presidential election was the waging of the Cold War.

_____8. When it became apparent that the Communist Chinese forces were winning the struggle for China, the response of the United States was full-scale military intervention in support of Chiang Kai-shek.

_____9. When General MacArthur called for a renewed offensive in Korea, President Truman decided to relieve the popular commander and bring him home.

_____10. The defection of the Dixiecrats from the Democratic party and the unpopularity of Truman's reform policies led to a Republican victory in the 1948 presidential election.

MULTIPLE CHOICE

Circle the one alternative that *best* completes the statement or answers the question.

1. Which of the following was not a major postwar issue between the United States and the Soviet Union?
   a. the division of Europe
   b. the division of spheres of influence in China
   c. postwar economic aid
   d. control of atomic weapons

2. With his Truman Doctrine speech President Truman hoped to
   a. "scare hell" out of Americans so they would support the policy of containment.
   b. "scare hell" out of the Russians to take advantage of the American atomic monopoly.
   c. provide economic assistance for the rebuilding of Europe.
   d. establish a western military alliance to "contain" communism.

3. The "containment" policy originated among
   a. members of the National Security Council.
   b. the leaders of the National Security Council.
   c. the Joint Chiefs of Staff.
   d. State Department leaders and experts.

4. How did the United States assure western Europeans that it would honor its NATO commitment?
   a. by sharing control of its atomic arsenal
   b. by stationing American troops in western Europe
   c. by signing a mutual defense pact
   d. all of the above

5. How did Truman respond to the Russian blockade of Berlin in 1948?
   a. by yielding to the blockade with a vigorous protest in the United Nations
   b. by airlifting supplies into the city
   c. by sending American tanks through the blockade
   d. by escalating the conflict with a counter blockade of Soviet positions

6. Which best describes the purposes of the Truman administration when it supported the National Security Act of 1947?
   a. to protect the country against internal threats to its security
   b. to unify the military services and coordinate diplomatic and military strategy
   c. to establish a western military alliance to contain communism
   d. to contain communism in the eastern Mediterranean by providing assistance to Greece and Turkey

7. The Marshall Plan was the plan to
   a. integrate the armed forces and create the National Security Council.
   b. finance the economic recovery of Europe.
   c. drive the Communist North Koreans from South Korea with military might.
   d. share the secrets of the atomic bomb with our allies.

8. The most significant result of the Korean War was
   a. massive rearmament by the United States.
   b. American determination to avoid land wars in Asia.
   c. the firing of General Douglas MacArthur.
   d. the unification of the military services.

9. The postwar mood of the American people could best be described as one that
   a. desired the extension of New Deal reforms into other areas.
   b. wished to back away from global efforts to halt the spread of communism.
   c. favored the retention of wartime price and wage controls.
   d. wanted the chance to buy more consumer goods; favored swift conversion to a peacetime economy; and called for higher wages.

10. McCarthy drew a disproportionate backing from which of the following groups?
    a. upper-middle-class businesspeople and professionals
    b. writers, teachers, artists, and other intellectuals
    c. working-class Irish, Polish, and Italian Catholics
    d. farmers, Hispanics, and African Americans

11. Why did Bernard Baruch and General Dwight David Eisenhower insist on preserving the American postwar monopoly on atomic weapons?
    a. to offset the Soviets' conventional military strength
    b. to intimidate the Russians in important diplomatic negotiations
    c. to turn back a Soviet plan for world conquest
    d. to balance the American government's budget by reducing defense costs

12. In 1945, the U.S. rejected the Russians' request for a reconstruction loan because it
    a. suspected the Russians would not repay.
    b. knew Russian did not need the money.
    c. wanted to retaliate for Russia's "iron curtain."

13. The principal goal of Eisenhower's policy was to
    a. liberate eastern Europe from communist control.
    b. relax tensions and initiate disarmament.
    c. prevent the fall of China to the Communists.
    d. win the arms race with a technological breakthrough.

14. How did President Eisenhower end the Korean War?
    a. by military offensive which gave the Chinese "one hell of a licking"
    b. by hinting that he might use nuclear weapons to end the military stalemate
    c. by making important concessions to the Chinese on the issue of Quemoy and Matsu
    d. all of the above

15. The result of the Army-McCarthy hearing was that
    a. McCarthy was publicly ridiculed and censured by the Senate.
    b. most of McCarthy's allegations were found to be accurate.
    c. McCarthy was subsequently tried and convicted of perjury.
    d. the Army responded by purging its ranks of revealed communists.

THOUGHT QUESTIONS

To check your understanding of the key issues of this period, solve the following problems:

1. Are the Soviet leaders expansionist because they are communists or because they are Russians?

2. Was the postwar policy of the Truman administration appropriate for the time and circumstances?

3. Does the American need for world markets best explain the origins of the Cold War?

4. How would you evaluate Truman's strengths and weaknesses as president? Did he accurately understand the American mood after World War II?

5. The existence of nuclear weapons played a very important role in the onset of the Cold War. True or false? Explain your answer.

6. How do you explain the anti-communist hysteria that gripped the U.S. during the McCarthy allegations? Can you compare it with other historical phenomena?

7. In light of recent upheavals in eastern Europe, can it be said that the Cold War is over?

CHAPTER 29

AFFLUENCE AND ANXIETY: FROM THE FAIR DEAL TO THE GREAT SOCIETY

SUMMARY
In postwar America, new affluence replaced the poverty and hunger of the Great Depression.

THE POSTWAR BOOM
An intensified demand for consumer goods and heavy government spending stimulated economic growth from the late 1940s through the 1950s. Although the rate of economic growth slowed in the second half of the 1950s, most Americans had far more real income during this era than ever before.

Postwar Prosperity
By 1950, production caught up with demand and the gross national product reached a point fifty percent higher than in 1940. The baby boom and expanding suburbia stimulated consumerism as fear of another depression dissipated. Slowdowns in economic growth occurred in the second half of the decade, but higher pay and shorter hours remained as permanent standards in the American workplace.

Life in the Suburbs
The newly affluent postwar generation shed their identities to live in look-alike homes and embrace the new culture of the suburbs. Life in these communities depended on the automobile. Homemaking and child rearing became primary vocations of suburban women.

THE GOOD LIFE?
Despite an abundance of material goods, many Americans questioned the quality of their lives.

Areas of Greatest Growth
Among the institutions that flourished in the postwar years was organized religion. A tremendous increase in the number of school-aged children created an enormous strain on local school districts. The number of young adults attending college increased precipitously. At home, television became the most popular entertainment medium-a safe conveyor of the consumer culture.

Critics of the Consumer Society
Critics like John Riesman, C. Wright Mills, and Jack Kerouac found fault with the blandness, conformity, corporate dehumanization, and the loss of individuality of the 1950s.

FAREWELL TO REFORM
Growing affluence removed the urgency for social and economic change.

Truman and the Fair Deal
In the wake of his 1948 electoral victory, President Truman tried to push for too many reforms too soon. Although he failed to get congressional and public support for the "Fair Deal," Truman's spirited efforts did prevent Republicans from repealing New Deal social legislation.

The Reaction to *Sputnik*
The Soviet launching of an orbiting satellite caused panic among the American people in 1957 and heightened concern and self-assessment that the nation had lost its unquestioned supremacy in the world.

Eisenhower's Modern Republicanism
When Dwight Eisenhower was elected in 1952, moderation based upon fiscal conservatism, encouragement of private initiative, and reduction of federal programs became the theme. His administration's legislative record (which consisted of extending Social Security benefits and creating the Department of Health, Education, and Welfare) was relatively modest. One significant accomplishment, the Highway Act of 1956, created the modern interstate system. Continued prosperity allowed Americans to accept increasing governmental spending and larger federal deficits

THE STRUGGLE OVER CIVIL RIGHTS
The Cold War helped to arouse national conscience in favor of civil rights for African Americans. Although benefitting economically from World War II, blacks continued to live in blighted neighborhoods and to be desegregated from white society.

Civil Rights as a Political Issue
Although President Truman had failed to push his civil rights package through Congress over southern opposition, he did succeed in adding civil rights to the liberal agenda, and most importantly, in segregating the armed forces.

Desegregating the Schools
The Supreme Court took the lead in reversing the late-nineteenth century's "separate but equal" decisions. In *Brown v. Board of Education of Topeka*, the Court ordered the nation's public schools to admit African American students for the first time. President Eisenhower sent troops into Little Rock, Arkansas to enforce the ruling but, on the whole, lack of presidential support weakened the desegregation process. A permanent Civil Rights Commission was established to protect voting rights, however.

The Beginnings of Black Activism
In Montgomery, Alabama, Rosa Parks and Dr. Martin Luther King, Jr., led a successful boycott against the city's segregated bus system. Drawing from sources such as Gandhi, King developed

the concept of passive resistance. In 1960, "sit-ins" and other demonstrations succeeded in desegregating many public facilities.

KENNEDY AND THE NEW FRONTIER
John F. Kennedy took advantage of television debates and a national sense of dissatisfaction to narrowly defeat the Republican candidate Richard Nixon for the presidency in 1960.

The New Frontiersmen
Kennedy's election marked the arrival of a new generation of leadership. The new administration reflected the president's youth and energy. Perhaps his greatest asset was his personality and style.

The Congressional Obstacle
Because the conservative coalition stood firmly against education and healthcare proposals, much of the New Frontier languished in Congress. Kennedy did win approval of a trade-expansion program and a slight increase in the minimum wage.

Economic Advance
The greatest stimulus to economic growth came from increased appropriations for defense and space. His chief economic advisor, Walter Heller, called for major tax cuts to stimulate consumer spending. Personal income and corporate profits increased dramatically.

Moving Slowly on Civil Rights
The president's solution to the problem of civil rights was to exert executive leadership rather than depend on congressional action. He supported the attempt by James Meredith to gain admission to the University of Mississippi over Governor Ross Barnett's opposition.

"I Have a Dream"
Responding to Dr. King's continued campaign for racial justice in Birmingham and his eloquent speech from the Lincoln Memorial in 1963, Kennedy decided to take the offensive and push for civil rights legislation. By the time of the president's death, his civil rights bills were well on their way to passage.

The Supreme Court and Reform
The Warren-led Court made far-reaching decisions that improved the rights of accused criminals, and brought about more equitable reapportionment in legislative redistricting. The activism of the Court stirred a storm of criticism.

"LET US CONTINUE"
VicePresident Lyndon Johnson moved quickly to fill the void left by Kennedy's death.

Johnson in Action
Although lacking Kennedy's charm and charisma, Johnson possessed far greater ability than his predecessor in dealing with Congress. He sought consensus rather than confrontation. He

succeeded in achieving passage of Kennedy's civil rights measures. The Civil Rights Act of 1964 was a landmark in the advance of American freedom and equality.

The Election of 1964
Convinced of the detrimental societal effects of poverty, Johnson declared an unconditional "war on poverty" and set up the new Office of Economic Opportunity. In 1964, Johnson soundly defeated the hawkish Republican Barry Goldwater and was elected to his own term in office.

The Triumph of Reform
Announcing his "Great Society," the president pushed for Medicare and Medicaid assistance and for federal aid to public education. The Voting Rights Act encouraged great increases in African American voter registration.

LEARNING OBJECTIVES

After mastering this chapter, you should be able to

1. Explain why Levittown was symptomatic of American conformity and consumerism of the postwar years.

2. Describe the problems of reconverting to a peacetime economy and the reasons for the surge of the economy after 1946.

3. Analyze the components of Truman's Fair Deal and establish the reasons why most of his package was not enacted.

4. Using specific references, explain why Eisenhower's administration marked an era of moderation.

5. Summarize the strengths and assets that President Kennedy brought into office.

6. Examine the programs of the New Frontier.

7. Discuss the objectives, victories, and failures of the civil rights movement in the 1950s.

8. Summarize the contributions of Martin Luther King, Jr., during the 1950s.

9. Identify the major accomplishments under Johnson's "Great Society."

10. Discuss the major obstacles to successful passage of such landmark legislative packages as Medicare and Medicaid, federal aid to public education, and the Civil Rights and Voting Rights Acts.

11. Explain the effects of suburban life on American families.

12. Determine why America said farewell to the New Deal spirit and the effect this had on Truman's presidency.

13. Define "modern Republicanism" as developed during the Eisenhower administration.

14. Identify the reasons why the pace of desegregation of the schools was slow.

15. Explain how Johnson's style and abilities contrasted with Kennedy's.

GLOSSARY

To build your social science vocabulary, familiarize yourself with the following terms:

1. **conformity** the tendency to correspond or behave alike. "They condemned the conformity, charging the newly affluent with forsaking traditional American individualism. . . ."

2. **affluence** material abundance or comfort. ". . . the American people had achieved an affluence that finally erased the lingering memories of the Great Depression."

3. **gross national product** the total sum of goods and services produced in a nation during a year. ". . . and the gross national product (GNP) reached $318 billion. . . ."

4. **real income** income after accounting for inflation. ". . . the average American family had twice as much real income to spend. . . ."

5. **disposable income** remaining income after taxes. ". . . per capita disposable income rose by $500. . . ."

6. **feminism** organized movement for political, economic, and social equality for women. "The nuclear family, typical of the suburb, did nothing to encourage the development of feminism."

7. **fiscal conservative** one who believes in minimal governmental interference with economic performance and limited government spending. "Ike was a fiscal conservative who was intent on balancing the budget."

8. **desegregation** the process of removing the characteristics of segregation, that is, of integrating or assimilating. "The process of desegregating the schools proved to be agonizingly slow."

9. **passive resistance** a posture or attitude of peaceful opposition or unwillingness to cooperate with authority. "Drawing on sources as diverse as Gandhi and Henry David Thoreau, King came out of the bus boycott with the concept of passive resistance."

10. **disfranchised** having been deprived of the franchise, that is, the right to vote. "To register previously disfranchised citizens. . . ."

11. **automation** technological system or apparatus that operates automatically" . . . industry installed electronic sensors and processors as it underwent extensive automation.

12. **neo-orthodoxy** a movement after World War II that affirmed the absolute sovereignty of God and challenged liberal theology" . . . the emergence of neo-orthodoxy in Protestant seminaries. . . ."

13. **suburbia** the social customs of suburban life. "A number of widely read books explored the flaws in the new suburbia."

14. **sit-ins** acts of protest involving remaining on the premises of an establishment that practices discrimination; a common practice during the civil rights movement. "Other students, both whites and blacks, joined in similar 'sit-ins' across the South . . ."

15. **recession** a downturn in the economic cycle characterized by stagnating economic growth and a usually higher rate of unemployment. "JFK was determined to recover quickly from the recession. . . ."

IDENTIFICATION

Briefly identify the meaning and significance of the following terms.

1. Levittown _____

   _____

2. baby boom _____

   _____

3. *Sputnik* _____

   _____

4. Highway Act of 1956 _____

   _____

5. Commission on Civil Rights _____

   _____

6. Brown v. Board of Education of Topeka _____

_____

7. Martin Luther King, Jr. _____

_____

8. Southern Christian Leadership Conference _____

_____

9. Fair Employment Practices Committee _____

_____

10. New Frontier _____

_____

MATCHING

A. Match the following Supreme Court decisions with the appropriate identification.

_____1. *Brown v. Board of Education*   **a.** defendants have to be provided with legal council

_____2. *Baker v. Carr*   **b.** defendants cannot be interrogated or induced to confess to a crime without legal counsel present

_____3. *Gideon v. Wainwright*   **c.** Tennessee had to redistribute its legislative seats to bring about equal representation or reapportionment

_____4. *Miranda v. Arizona*   **d.** separate educational facilities for the races are inherently unequal

_____5. *Escobedo v. Illinois*   **e.** the right of a woman to have an abortion cannot be deprived by state laws

f. defendants must be informed of their constitutional rights

B. Match the following writers with the appropriate description.

_____1. Jack Kerouac

_____2. C. Wright Mills

_____3. David Riesman

_____4. John Keats

_____5. Katherine Gordon

a. bemoaned the "gimme" kids suburbia produced

b. founded the "beats," a literary group that rejected the materialistic 1950s

c. recognized the depersonalizing aspects of the office and targeted the corporation as the villain of modern America

d. described suburban America as having identical boxes inhabited by the Drones and Amiables

e. said that the 1950s produced the "other-directed" consumer society, which lacked individuality and creativity

f. condemned the racial hostility that the all-white suburbs created

COMPLETION

Answer the question or complete the statement by filling in the blanks with the correct word or words.

1. Levitt answered the postwar American desire to move to _____, away from the central city.

2. In response to the launch of *Sputnik* and to compete with the Russians in the space race, Congress created the _____.

3. Although most of his civil rights initiatives were thwarted, Truman was successful in ordering the desegregation of the _____.

4. To restore tranquility to a divided nation, the Eisenhower administration had a theme of _____.

5. To achieve civil rights goals, Dr. Martin Luther King, Jr., used the tactic of _____ to appeal to middle-class America.

6. The highway trust fund created under the Highway Act of 1956 helped subsidize the _____.

7. The _____, an extreme anti-Communist, conservative group of the 1950s and 1960s, demanded the impeachment of Chief Justice Earl Warren.

8. The philosophy Martin Luther King, Jr., borrowed from Gandhi and applied to the civil rights movement was _____.

9. In the South, racial _____ was enforced at all places of public entertainment.

TRUE/FALSE

Mark the following statements either T (True) or F (False).

____1. During the decade of the 1950s, population growth in the inner city kept pace with the growth of suburbia.

____2. By 1960, one-fourth of all existing homes had been built since 1950.

____3. With more men entering the workforce after the war, the number of wives working outside the home decreased.

____4. Eisenhower claimed that when it came to money he was liberal, and when it came to human beings he was conservative.

____5. Reflecting the basic conservative attitudes of the 1960s, the Warren Court issued several decisions that assisted prosecutors and police in the war against crime.

____6. Although President Truman failed to achieve significant civil rights legislation, he succeeded in pushing the issue to the forefront of the political agenda.

____7. One of the most important new directions undertaken by American youth between 1940 and 1960 was away from college education toward technical-vocational training and early entry into the job market.

____8. Michael Harrington's book *The Other America* asserted that poverty was widespread, but generally invisible, in America and that many of the poor were trapped in the same culture of poverty as their parents.

____9. According to C. Wright Mills, the modern office was even more dehumanizing than the industrial assembly line.

____10. The American desire to enter the space race was a logical result of technological evolution and had very little to do with Cold War feelings or competition with the Russians.

MULTIPLE CHOICE

Circle the one alternative that *best* completes the statement or answers the question.

1. An accurate description of the social makeup of the suburbs is that
   a. only middle-class people lived there.
   b. they mainly attracted professional types such as doctors and lawyers.
   c. a surprising variety of practically all economic types—excluding mainly the very rich and very poor—resided there.
   d. only the very rich could afford to live there.

2. The attitude of most Americans toward further political and social reforms after the war was that
   a. because of newly acquired affluence, they turned away from reforms.
   b. they realized that, especially in civil rights, a great deal of work needed to be done.
   c. they expected President Truman to continue the economic reforms of the New Deal tradition.
   d. they usually supported only reforms for the advantage of labor.

3. President Truman's legislative program, the Fair Deal, called for
   a. measures opposed to the strengthening of labor unions.
   b. dismantling most of the legislated social gains of the New Deal.
   c. national medical insurance, federal aid to education, and civil rights advances, and the desegregation of the armed forces.
   d. significant tax cuts, elimination of wartime restrictions, and subsidies for business expansion.

4. The Student Nonviolent Coordinating Committee was responsible for
   a. coordinating student protests against the war in Vietnam.
   b. bolstering the sagging fortunes of the NAACP by joining it in the struggle for civil rights.
   c. direct but peaceful confrontation that would heighten the social tension of the civil rights movement.
   d. opposing the efforts of the Southern Christian Leadership Conference.

5. John F. Kennedy took advantage of which of the following factors to win the presidency in 1960?
   a. the sagging national economy and the frustration over *Sputnik*
   b. his greater name recognition than Nixon's
   c. his prior reputation for being a strong civil rights crusader
   d. his reputation for being a tougher cold warrior than Nixon

6. Johnson's Great Society represented
   a. conservative support for corporations and wealthy Americans.
   b. an intensifying of the war effort in Vietnam.
   c. extensive tax cuts and defense spending cuts.
   d. long-awaited reforms in health care, federal aid to education, and promotion of civil rights.

7. Eisenhower's decision to send troops into Little Rock, Arkansas, was in response to
   a. a violent strike of railroad workers.
   b. a direct challenge to the Supreme Court decision in *Brown v. Board of Education of Topeka* when the Governor of Arkansas used armed troops to turn back African American students in their attempt to attend school.
   c. student protests against the war in Korea.
   d. the beatings of "freedom ride" protesters by local Klansmen and other toughs.

8. *Brown v. Board of Education of Topeka* determined that
   a. separate educational facilities for the races had to be eliminated.
   b. property owners had to pay school taxes even if they did not have children attending school.
   c. busing could be used to achieve racial balance in the schools.
   d. private schools could continue to bar minority applicants.

9. The main purpose of the Southern Christian Leadership Conference was to
   a. unite conservative religious denominations in the South against federal intrusion into local racial affairs.
   b. settle some of the outstanding theological differences still existing among American churches.
   c. direct the movement against segregation and promote peaceful confrontation against the enemies of racial equality.
   d. educate aspiring religious leaders to the need for moral leadership in the coming years.

10. The Soviet launching of *Sputnik* revealed in America a
    a. haunting insecurity and growing apprehension about our priorities and our competitive edge.
    b. prolonged paralysis and a desire to retreat from further confrontation with the Soviets.
    c. passive naivete and apathy to international issues.
    d. continued self-confidence that we would dominate the future as we had the previous decade.

11. The main bloc of voters that contributed to the election of Truman in 1948 consisted of
    a. professional and white-collar workers.
    b. businessmen and unorganized labor.
    c. federal workers and suburban middle class.
    d. farmers, organized labor, African Americans, and other minorities.

12. The Taft-Hartley Act
    a. gave workers the right of collective bargaining.
    b. repealed the 1935 Wagner Act.
    c. outlawed "closed shop" and other unfair labor practices.
    d. was supported by Truman.

13. All of the following were consequences of suburban living after World War II except
    a. encouragement for feminism.
    b. greater loss of intimate contact with uncles, aunts, and grandparents.
    c. a new affluence replacing the deprivation of the Great Depression.
    d. fulfillment of the desire for more space, comfort, and freedom of action.

14. Eisenhower's method of dealing with Congress during his administration was to
    a. lobby with intensity for needed reform legislation.
    b. challenge them to take the lead in civil rights activism.
    c. urge Congress to expand its authority over such issues as education, health care, and the federal budget.
    d. remain insulated from most legislative issues, preferring to play a passive role.

15. Most of the actual stimulation of the economy during the Kennedy administration came from
    a. increased social welfare programs.
    b. tax increases to increase federal spending.
    c. the lifting of wage and price controls held over from the Eisenhower years.
    d. greatly increased appropriations for defense and space.

THOUGHT QUESTIONS

To check your understanding of the key issues of this period, solve the following problems:

1. What were some of the sociological effects of suburban living after the war?

2. What was Martin Luther King, Jr., pressing for with passive resistance and civil disobedience? Why were his tactics successful?

3. In what ways were Kennedy's New Frontier and Johnson's Great Society continuations of the New Deal? How were they different?

4. What factors enabled the civil rights movement to achieve some successes under the apparently conservative administration of Eisenhower?

5. According to William H. Whyte, David Riesman, and C. Wright Mills, what was disturbingly flawed about life in the 1950s? Were their concerns justified? Why or why not?

6. How would you describe the postwar mood of Americans, and why was this mood more reflected in the Eisenhower presidency than in that of Truman?

CHAPTER 30

VIETNAM AND THE ESCALATING COLD WAR, 1953-1968

SUMMARY
When the Viet Minh drove the French from Dien Bien Phu, Eisenhower decided to sponsor the Diem regime in the South rather than support elections throughout the partitioned country, as called for by the Geneva Conference. Under Kennedy and Johnson, the continued American involvement in Vietnam led to escalation and, eventually, stalemate.

EISENHOWER WAGES THE COLD WAR
Eisenhower directed his considerable political and diplomatic skills toward a relaxation of Cold War tensions while letting Secretary Dulles's hard-line speeches placate Republican extremists.

Containing China
The president chose to oppose China forcefully to contain communist expansion in Asia and, at the same time, to drive a wedge between China and Russia. Chinese shelling of Quemoy and Matsu tested the administration's resolve.

Turmoil in the Middle East
In the Middle East, Eisenhower ended the Suez crisis, with the United States replacing the English as the leading Western power in the area, then used restrained force to resolve a crisis in Lebanon.

Covert Actions
In Iran, Guatemala, and Cuba, the president relied on covert actions that revealed his "corrupting belief that the ends justified the means."

Waging Peace
To reduce U.S.-U.S.S.R. tensions, Eisenhower attempted to end the arms race with an "open skies" proposal and suspension of nuclear testing, but Russia's post-*Sputnik* belligerence and the U-2 fiasco aborted his initiative. Eisenhower had begun a process of relaxing tensions, but his distrust of communism and Khrushchev's belligerence led to its failure.

KENNEDY INTENSIFIES THE COLD WAR
In foreign affairs John Kennedy surrounded himself with the "best and brightest," young, aggressive advisers determined to invoke a hard-line approach to the Soviet Union. The new administration supported containment and authorized a massive buildup of nuclear weapons.

Flexible Response
Kennedy also launched two new strategies: to give America the flexible response needed to meet any challenge, and to create a successful first-strike capability.

Crisis over Berlin
A "superpower" stalemate that developed in Berlin left Germany divided between the East and the West. Kennedy ordered further military spending for weaponry to demonstrate American determination to honor its international commitments.

Containing Fidel Castro
Kennedy gave his approval to a CIA plan to topple Castro by using Cuban exiles as invasion troops. The Bay of Pigs landing proved to be an utter disaster, and Kennedy took responsibility for the failure.

At the Brink
In 1962 the United States faced a much more serious issue regarding Soviet installation of nuclear missiles in Cuba. Kennedy refused to bargain on the missiles and boldly ordered a quarantine of Cuba as the world braced for a possible nuclear showdown. Premier Khrushchev backed down, but the Russians went on a crash nuclear buildup to achieve parity with the United States. Some positive results followed: a limited test ban treaty signed in 1963, a hot line to speed communication between the nuclear antagonists, a policy of conciliation replacing that of confrontation. Those gains were offset by a dramatic escalation in the arms race.

JOHNSON ESCALATES THE VIETNAM WAR
Lyndon Johnson shared Kennedy's Cold War view and inherited his military and diplomatic problems. His forcefulness in opposing Castro and the Latin American left brought increasing criticism from many directions, as did his resolve to contain communism in Southeast Asia.

Civil War in Vietnam
In Vietnam the United States had supported the South Vietnamese regime of Ngo Dinh Diem against communist insurgents. Kennedy had sent military advisors and substantial military and economic aid. Full-scale American involvement began under Johnson in 1965, after the Gulf of Tonkin resolution by Congress gave the president the power to take the offensive.

Escalation
Refusing to call for an invasion of the North, Johnson opted for a massive escalation. As his "open-ended commitment" to force a diplomatic solution on Hanoi intensified, American combat missions in the South and air strikes against the North increased. But Johnson refused to admit that he had committed the U.S. to full-scale military involvement, and the situation in Southeast Asia worsened.

Stalemate
Despite massive American escalation, the war remained stalemated in 1968 when the surprising force of the communists' Tet offensive discredited American military leaders and led President

Johnson to forego further escalation, open up peace negotiations with Hanoi, then withdraw from his bid for reelection.

LEARNING OBJECTIVES

After mastering this chapter, you should be able to

1. Describe and evaluate the principal changes in foreign policy initiated by Eisenhower.

2. Evaluate Eisenhower's handling of the French request for American intervention in Indochina.

3. Describe and evaluate Eisenhower's response to the Suez and Lebanese crises.

4. Describe and evaluate Eisenhower's use of the CIA and covert actions in Iran, Guatemala, and Cuba.

5. Trace Eisenhower's efforts at control of nuclear arms from April 1953 through his last speech as president.

6. Analyze Kennedy's attitude toward the Cold War and nuclear armaments and the possible long-term consequences vis-a-vis the Soviet Union.

7. Summarize the main events and results of the Bay of Pigs landing and the Cuban missile crisis.

8. Compare and contrast the arguments for continued confrontation or conciliation with the Russians in the context of the Cuban missile crisis.

9. Understand the reasons for America's buildup of military strength in Vietnam and how this escalation undermined the Johnson administration.

10. Describe the escalation of America's involvement in the Vietnam War from 1965 to 1968.

11. Explain why and how the year 1968 seemed to mark a turning point in the Vietnam War.

GLOSSARY

To build your social science vocabulary, familiarize yourself with the following terms:

1. **guerrilla** irregular military forces. "The French hoped to engage the elusive guerrilla forces. . . ."

2. **tactical** maneuvered or positioned for military advantage. "The French were in a hopeless tactical position. . . ."

3. **coup** a very successful move. "[A]n unexpected nationalist coup overthrew the pro-Western government of Iraq...."

4. **subversion** attempt to undermine or overthrow. "Yet his reliance on coups and subversion... reveal Ike's corrupting belief that the ends justified the means."

5. **surveillance** a watch, supervision or observation. "'Open skies'... would overcome the... Russian objection by having both countries open their territory to aerial surveillance."

6. **military-industrial complex** military and industrial elites promoting defense spending and a militaristic foreign policy. "[W]e must guard against the acquisition of unwarranted influence ... by the military-industrial complex...."

7. **first strike** a nuclear offensive rather than defensive. "The United States thus opened a missile gap in reverse, creating the possibility of a successful American first strike."

8. **counterinsurgency** organized military and intelligence activity designed to prevent, control, or detect insurrection. "The president took a personal interest in counterinsurgency."

9. **quarantine** a blockade or restraint. "He would proclaim a quarantine of Cuba to prevent the arrival of new missiles...."

10. **conciliation** agreement or compromise. "... he shifted from the rhetoric of confrontation to that of conciliation...."

11. **hawks** those who support war or militancy. "Hawks who had backed Kennedy's military buildup felt that events had justified a policy of nuclear superiority."

12. **junta** a group of people, usually military, in control of a government after a military coup. "When a military junta overthrew a leftist regime in Brazil...."

13. **covert** secretive, unannounced or unofficial. "... he expanded American support for covert actions...."

14. **escalation** buildup or increase. "... critics charged that LBJ wanted a blank check from Congress to carry out the future escalation of the Vietnam War...."

15. **interdiction** bombardment to hinder an enemy's progress. "Nor were the efforts at interdiction any more successful."

IDENTIFICATION

Briefly identify the meaning and significance of the following terms.

1. Dien Bien Phu

2. John Foster Dulles

3. Quemoy and Matsu

4. Suez crisis

5. covert actions

6. Berlin Wall

7. Bay of Pigs

8. Cuban missile crisis

9. Gulf of Tonkin affair

10. escalation

MATCHING

A. Match the following Cold War leaders with the appropriate description.

____1. Mao Tse-tung

____2. Ho Chi Minh

____3. Nikita Khrushchev

____4. Ngo Dinh Diem

____5. Gamal Nasser

a. Lebanese leader supported by Eisenhower

b. Chinese Communist who won control of Chinese mainland

c. Egyptian leader who seized the Suez Canal

d. Soviet leader who intensified the Cold War

e. Vietnamese who led a successful civil war against the French

f. South Vietnamese leader sponsored by Eisenhower

B. Match the following public figures with the appropriate description.

____1. Dean Rusk

____2. Robert McNamara

____3. McGeorge Bundy

____4. Robert F. Kennedy

____5. Hubert Humphrey

a. secretary of state, appointed by Kennedy, who said during the Cuban missile crisis, "We're eyeball to eyeball, and I think the other fellow just blinked"

b. MIT economist who became one of Kennedy's most important advisers

c. president of Ford Motor Company who became secretary of defense

d. U.S. Attorney General and Kennedy's most controversial cabinet appointee

e. one of the "best and the brightest" who became Kennedy's national security adviser

f. vice-president under Johnson

COMPLETION

Answer the question or complete the statement by filling in the blanks with the correct word or words.

1. The 1960 Paris summit conference was aborted by the _____ incident.

2. In 1958 Eisenhower ordered American marines into the strategic Middle Eastern country of _____.

3. Khrushchev intensified the Cold War when Americans feared the Russians had achieved a technological breakthrough with _____.

4. The New Frontiersmen appointed by Kennedy were later referred to by journalist David Halberstam as _____

5. The purpose of the new military buildup was, according to Defense Secretary Robert McNamara, strategically to create _____.

6. The huge economic aid program called for by Kennedy for Latin America was the _____.

7. South Vietnamese rebels against the regime of Ngo Dinh Diem were known as _____.

8. After the Cuban missile crisis, President Kennedy and Premier Khrushchev agreed to install a _____ for instant communication to prevent any emergency.

9. Senator William Fulbright criticized Johnson's foreign policy and the fallacies of containment with his publication of _____.

10. Johnson complained that the Vietnam conflict, that "bitch of a war," would destroy "the woman I really loved—the _____.

TRUE/FALSE

Mark the following statements either T (True) or F (False).

_____1. In his last speech as president, Eisenhower warned of the growing power of a "military industrial complex."

_____2. Because of his lack of experience in American politics, Eisenhower was a poorly prepared Cold War leader.

_____3. In 1954, Eisenhower rejected American intervention in Vietnam because he feared American troops would be "swallowed up" and because he did not want to compromise the American "tradition of anticolonialism."

_____4. The United States opposed elections to reunite Vietnam in 1956 because it feared Ho Chi Minh would win.

_____5. The nuclear objective of the Kennedy administration was to concentrate primarily on defensive weapons.

_____6. Regarding the Bay of Pigs debacle, Kennedy took personal responsibility for the failure.

_____7. Following President Kennedy's response to the Berlin crisis, America claimed complete victory as the Soviets withdrew their occupation army from Berlin.

_____8. After the Cuban missile crisis, the Soviet Union recognized American nuclear superiority and concentrated primarily on conventional weapons.

_____9. John Kennedy's Alliance for Progress emphasized military rather than economic means in our Latin American policy.

_____10. "Strategic hamlets" were fire bases in South Vietnam from which American troops launched their operations.

MULTIPLE CHOICE

Circle the one alternative that *best* completes the statement or answers the question.

1. Which best describes the role played by John Foster Dulles in the conduct of foreign policy during the Eisenhower administration?
   a. He made most of the major decisions.
   b. He placated Republican extremists with his hard-line views.
   c. He was only a symbol for morality in policy.
   d. He worked behind the scenes, letting the president take credit for policy.

2. The principal goal of Eisenhower's policy was to
   a. liberate Europe from communist control.
   b. relax tensions and initiate disarmament.
   c. prevent the fall of China to communism.
   d. win the arms race with a technological breakthrough.

3. How did Eisenhower respond to the attempt by the French and English to seize the Suez Canal in 1956?
   a. by calling for their withdrawal
   b. by supporting them diplomatically but not militarily
   c. by supporting them with a naval blockade of Egypt
   d. by sending American ships to the canal to end the fighting

4. As an American Cold War leader, Eisenhower demonstrated
   a. an unwillingness to deal with the essentials of foreign policy.
   b. a decided preference for domestic rather than foreign policy.
   c. a willingness to seek peace and disarmament while supporting coups to overthrow unfriendly governments.
   d. a decided preference for military rather than diplomatic means in dealing with the Soviets.

5. The approach of the Kennedy administration toward defense spending and the nuclear arsenal was to
   a. cut back on spending and reduce the number of nuclear weapons.
   b. construct an awesome nuclear arsenal with first-strike capability, which would put the Soviets on the defensive.
   c. hold steady on defense spending but concentrate on conventional rather than nuclear weapons.
   d. carry the Eisenhower approach forward, balancing conventional with nuclear weapons.

6. The standoff between the Soviet Union and the United States over Berlin in 1961 had the following result
   a. The Berlin Wall would at last be torn down.
   b. The two nations agreed to reduce their nuclear weapons arsenal and share in the solution of the Berlin problem.
   c. The Soviet Union agreed to abandon all of Berlin, leaving the city in the hands of the Western powers.
   d. The tension gradually eased, but Berlin and the rest of Europe remained divided with neither side claiming complete victory.

7. President Kennedy's solution to the escalating guerrilla fighting in South Vietnam was to
   a. demand the overthrow of the oppressive Diem government.
   b. send thousands of American offensive ground forces to stabilize the region.
   c. continue to support Diem while recognizing that it was ultimately South Vietnam's war to win or lose.
   d. order the first large-scale bombings of North Vietnam.

8. The result of the Cuban missile crisis was that
   a. Khrushchev agreed to remove the missiles in return for the U.S. promise not to invade Cuba.
   b. the United States agreed to allow only defensive nuclear weapons in Cuba.
   c. the Communist government in Cuba collapsed and was replaced by a pro-American republic.
   d. the Soviet Union and the United States broke off all diplomatic and commercial relations.

9. Kennedy responded to Soviet missiles in Cuba by
   a. an invasion of Cuba to seize the missile sites.
   b. an air raid to destroy the missile sites.
   c. a naval occupation of the Cuban port through which Russian missiles and parts passed.
   d. a naval quarantine of Cuba to prevent the shipment of new missiles coupled with nuclear threat to force the removal of missiles already in place.

10. The Gulf of Tonkin Resolution resulted in
    a. a declaration of war by Congress on North Vietnam.
    b. Congress's support of Johnson's desire to increase military activity in Vietnam.
    c. the decision to bomb Hanoi and other North Vietnamese locations.
    d. the decision to overthrow the Diem regime.

11. Johnson's failure regarding Vietnam was to
    a. refuse to acknowledge he had committed the U.S. to dangerous military involvement.
    b. begin the process of sending military specialists and equipment into Vietnam.
    c. support the Diem regime.
    d. overstep the president's authority concerning military commitment.

12. Which best describes the Viet Cong?
    a. pro-American elements of the South Vietnamese military
    b. the South Vietnamese regular army
    c. the North Vietnamese regular army
    d. communist guerrillas in South Vietnam

13. Both the Kennedy and Johnson administrations developed a foreign policy based primarily on
    a. their Cold War views.
    b. a strong commitment to the United Nations.
    c. emerging theories of detente.
    d. a strong commitment to disarmament.

14. Lyndon Johnson used 20,000 American troops to intervene in
    a. Cuba.
    b. the Dominican Republic.
    c. Mexico.
    d. Argentina.

15. Which of the following events took place during the Johnson administration?
    a. the Tet offensive
    b. the Bay of Pigs invasion
    c. the U-2 incident
    d. all of the above

THOUGHT QUESTIONS

To check your understanding of the key issues of this period, solve the following problems:

1. Were the Eisenhower Cold War policies appropriate for the time and circumstances? Were those policies contradictory? On the whole, were they successful?

2. Given John Kennedy's military and foreign policy views, would he have followed the Vietnam policies pursued by Lyndon Johnson? Would he have escalated? Withdrawn?

3. How do the diplomatic events of the Kennedy administration indicate his commitment to the Cold War?

4. After considering the alternatives, do you think that Kennedy responded correctly to the Cuban missile crisis? What were the long-term consequences of that showdown?

5. Did the Latin American policies of Eisenhower, Kennedy, and Johnson differ significantly? Explain your answer.

6. How do you account for the buildup of American forces in Vietnam? To what degree was Johnson responsible for the tragedy of Vietnam?

CHAPTER 31

A CRISIS IN CONFIDENCE, 1965–1980

SUMMARY

YEARS OF TURMOIL

The Student Revolt
From 1964 to 1968, college students demonstrated for free speech and against war, racism, and poverty. The Students for a Democratic Society (SDS) recruited new members at campuses across the nation to protest America's deepening involvement in Vietnam.

The Cultural Revolution
Whereas political protests affected only a small proportion of the nation's youth, a far greater number of students rebelled against cultural conformity, seeking liberation with new fashions, music, and lifestyles.

"Black Power"
The failure of the civil rights movement to match legislative successes with economic advances for African Americans sparked militant attitudes and urban riots. Dr. Martin Luther King's insistence on nonviolence and peaceful integration was replaced by Stokely Carmichael's cries for "black power" and ethnic separation.

Ethnic Nationalism
In contrast to acceptance of the "melting pot" image of the United States, members of various ethnic groups demanded respect for and recognition of their unique heritages and contributions. César Chávez stirred the consciousness of Mexican Americans with his successful unionization of poorly paid migrant farm workers in California.

Women's Liberation
Feminists sought women's liberation from male chauvinism and domination. Betty Friedan attacked prevailing stereotypes of women as contented housekeepers in *The Feminine Mystique* (1963) and founded the National Organization for Women (NOW) in 1966. The Civil Rights Act of 1964 prohibited discrimination in employment on the basis of sex, and in 1972 Congress approved an Equal Rights Amendment to the Constitution which was never ratified by the states.

THE RETURN OF RICHARD NIXON

The Democrats Divide
Following the Tet offensive and a near political upset in the New Hampshire presidential primary, Lyndon B. Johnson withdrew from a reelection bid in early 1968. The assassination of Robert Kennedy in June 1968 virtually guaranteed Vice President Hubert Humphrey's nomination, but the bitter protests and violent police repression outside the Democratic convention in Chicago appalled the nation and exposed serious rifts in the party.

The Republican Resurgence
Stressing a return to the traditional values of law and order, Richard M. Nixon captured the Republican nomination and won a narrow election victory over Humphrey.

Nixon in Power
While Nixon appeared more moderate and restrained than in the past, he remained exceptionally sensitive to critism. He assembled a powerful White House staff whose main task was to shield him from Congress and the press.

Reshaping the Great Society
Nixon streamlined the federal bureaucracy. He also appointed conservative judges to the Supreme Court and shifted the responsibility for school integration to the federal courts as part of his "southern strategy" to build a Republican majority for 1972.

Nixonomics
Nixon inherited severe economic problems that did not seem to respond to traditional remedies. In 1971, however, he curbed inflation with a series of temporary wage and price freezes and improved the balance of trade with a devaluation of the dollar and a 10 percent surtax on imports.

Building a Republican Majority
Republicans sought to win new voters among traditionally Democratic blue-collar workers and southern whites for 1972. Vice President Spiro Agnew blamed Democratic liberals for such national social problems as drug abuse, sexual permissiveness, and crime in the streets.

In Search of Détente
Strongly influenced by National Security Adviser Henry Kissinger, Nixon pursued a foreign policy of détente—a relaxation of tension—with the Soviet Union. A Strategic Arms Limitation Talks (SALT) treaty was signed in 1972, followed by American sales of grain and computer technology to the Soviet Union.

Ending the Vietnam War
Secret negotiations between Kissinger and North Vietnam's Le Duc Tho produced a truce, signed in January 1973. Accepting what amounted to a disguised surrender, the United States agreed to remove its troops in return for the release of all American prisoners of war.

THE CRISIS OF DEMOCRACY

The Politics of Deceit
The Nixon administration's inordinate fear of political enemies led to numerous illegal activities by Republican officials and campaign supporters, including plans to break into the Democratic national headquarters in the Watergate building.

The Election of 1972
Ironically, the Watergate break-in was hardly necessary to guarantee an overwhelming reelection victory for Nixon in 1972. The Democrats nominated George McGovern, a candidate perceived as too liberal by most Americans. George Wallace withdrew from the campaign after an attempted assassination, leaving Nixon with a monopoly on conservative voters.

The Watergate Scandal
It took over two years of painstaking investigation to reveal the president's attempt to cover up the involvement of White House aides. After the House Judiciary Committee voted three articles of impeachment and the Supreme Court ordered the release of the tapes of presidential conversations, Nixon chose to resign on August 9, 1974. The revelation of the truth confirmed the efficacy of the American political system, but severely shook the public's faith in the nation's political leadership.

ENERGY AND THE ECONOMY

The October War
In October 1973, Arab nations imposed an oil embargo against the United States to force American pressure on Israel to return Arab lands. Henry Kissinger soon negotiated an end to the embargo, but dramatic increases in oil prices remained and alerted Americans to an energy crisis.

The Oil Shocks
Increased energy costs led to double-digit inflation, rising unemployment, and a decline in economic growth for the United States. In 1979, the Organization of Petroleum Exporting Countries (OPEC) took advantage of the Iranian Revolution to embark on a new round of oil price increases.

The Search for an Energy Policy
Congress could not agree on a coherent energy policy. Republicans advocated removal of price controls and increased production while the Democrats wished to maintain price controls and pursue conservation efforts.

The Great Inflation
The startling price increases of the 1970s resulted from swollen deficits from the Vietnam War, a worldwide shortage of food, and especially the sixfold increase in oil prices. Wages for many Americans failed to keep pace and actions by the Federal Reserve Board increased interest rates.

The Shifting American Economy
The United States lost world markets though the 1970s in heavy industries, such as steel and automobiles. The more diversified multinational corporations and conglomerates fared better. Within the United States, industry shifted increasingly to the Sunbelt, with high-technology industries as computer and electronics firms proving most profitable.

POLITICS AFTER WATERGATE

The Ford Administration
Ford's popularity rapidly declined with a pardon of Nixon and a seeming ineptitude in dealing with Congress. When Congressional investigations reveled excesses by the CIA, Ford approved reform of the agency and appointed George Bush as its new director.

The 1976 Campaign
Former Georgia Governor Jimmy Carter won the Democratic nomination by portraying himself as an honest and candid "outsider," untainted by Washington politics. Carter won a narrow victory, ensured by overwhelming support from African American voters.

Disenchantment with Carter
Although an intelligent politician and a master of symbols, Carter seemed to lack a clear sense of direction. Tension and conflict among his officials and priorities doomed the administration to failure.

FROM DÉTENTE TO RENEWED COLD WAR

Retreat in Asia
In 1974, Congress cut military aid to South Vietnam and refused to grant additional aid the next year as Communists seized control.

Accommodation in Latin America
Carter signed two treaties in 1977 providing a gradual return of the Panama Canal and zone to Panama by the end of the century. Carter held out the lure of American economic aid in hopes of moderating the leftist Sandinista regime in Nicaragua as well as the right wing military junta in El Salvador. Neither venture proved successful.

The Quest for Peace in the Middle East
The Camp David accords of 1978 led ultimately to a peace treaty between Egypt and Israel, but left the problems of the Palestinian Arabs unsettled. In 1979, Iranian mobs in Teheran seized the American embassy and fifty-eight American hostages. The failure of diplomacy, economic reprisals, and a military rescue mission to free the hostages steadily eroded the nation's confidence in Carter's leadership.

The Cold War Resumes
When the Soviets invaded Afghanistan in December 1979, Carter banned sales of grain and high-tech equipment to the Soviet Union, reinstated registration for the draft, and ordered a boycott of the 1980 Moscow Olympics. These actions failed to force Russia out of Afghanistan and signalled a resumption of the Cold War.

LEARNING OBJECTIVES

After mastering this chapter, you should be able to

1. Analyze why and how the 1960s became a decade of social and political protests as well as cultural revolution.

2. Assess the impacts made by the following protest groups: (a) college students, (b) African American militants, (c) Mexican Americans, and (d) women's liberation groups.

3. Discuss the reasons for Democratic division and Republican resurgence in the election of 1968.

4. Explain Nixon's first-term goals and accomplishments in domestic as well as foreign affairs.

5. Assess the impact of the Watergate controversy on the American political system.

6. describe the causes of the energy crisis as well as its impact on the American economy and political scene.

7. Compare and contrast the approaches taken by Presidents Ford and Carter to correct America's economic problems.

8. Explain the factors contributing to Jimmy Carter's victory over Gerald Ford in the election of 1976.

9. Account for the public disenchantment with Carter that resulted in his one-term presidency.

10. Analyze Carter's successes and failures in dealing with foreign affairs.

GLOSSARY

To build your social science vocabulary, familiarize yourself with the following terms:

1. **manifesto** a public declaration of views. ". . . Port Huron Statement, a manifesto of the newly organized Students for a Democratic Society (SDS). . . . "

2. **rhetoric** insincere or exaggerated language. "Many women were repelled by the harsh rhetoric of the extremists. . . ."

3. **epithets** disparaging or abusive words. "Epithets and cries of 'pigs' brought about a savage response from Daley's police. . . ."

4. **debacle** breakdown; collapse. "The primary beneficiary of the Democratic debacle was Richard Nixon."

5. **penchant** strong leaning or tendency. "Gone was the fiery rhetoric and the penchant for making enemies. . . ."

6. **détente** a relaxation of strained tensions or relations. "Nixon and Kissinger shrewdly played the China card as their first step toward achieving détente . . . with the Soviet Union."

7. **quagmire** soft quicksand that yields under the foot but drags one down. "After eight years of fighting, the United States had emerged from the quagmire in Southeast Asia."

8. **stonewall** to engage in obstructive debate or delaying tactics. "[Nixon said to John Mitchell] 'I want you all to stonewall it. . . .'"

9. **executive privilege** authority of the president to refuse to divulge conversations among members of the executive branch, presumably to provide protection on matters of national security. "At first the president tried to invoke executive privilege to withhold the tapes".

10. **embargo** governmental order prohibiting outgoing shipments. "The Arab oil embargo had a disastrous effect on the American economy."

11. **cartel** a combination of independent enterprisers to restrict competition and establish a monopoly. ". . . members of the OPEC cartel took advantage of the situation to raise prices. . . ."

12. **self-effacing** retiring, placing oneself in the background. "The new president, described by an associate as 'superficially self-effacing but intensely shrewd,' was an ambitious and intelligent politician."

13. **consensus** group solidarity or agreement in sentiment or belief. "The new national consensus was symbolized by the War Powers Act. . . ."

14. **reactionary** conservative; marked by movement back to a former or outmoded policy or condition. ". . . Central America, where the United States had imposed order for most of the twentieth century by backing reactionary regimes."

15. **autonomy** quality or state of being self-governing. ". . . the Camp David accords dealt gingerly with the problem of Palestinian autonomy in the West Bank and Gaza Strip areas."

IDENTIFICATION

Briefly identify the meaning and significance of the following terms.

1. Robert F. Kennedy _____

_____

2. George Wallace _____

_____

3. Henry Kissinger _____

_____

4. Warren Burger _____

_____

5. the Pentagon Papers _____

_____

6. OPEC _____

_____

7. Gerald R. Ford_____

_____

8. the Mayaguez _____

_____

9. Camp David accords _____

_____

10. the hostage crisis _____

_____

MATCHING

A. Match the following activists of the 1960s with the appropriate description.

____1. Mario Savio
a. student leader of the Free Speech Movement at the University of California at Berkeley

____2. Bob Dylan
b. feminist author and founder of the National Organization for Women (NOW)

____3. Stokely Carmichael
c. leader of the Yippie movement who mocked the consumer culture

____4. César Chávez
d. African American leader calling for "black power" and racial pride

____5. Betty Friedan
e. musician popular for songs of social protest

f. Mexican American labor leader who organized migrant farm workers in California

B. Match the following Watergate figures with the appropriate description.

____1. John J. Sirica
a. Attorney General and head of Nixon's reelection committee later receiving a jail term for his role in Watergate

____2. John Dean
b. Watergate special prosecutor, fired by Nixon for demanding release of presidential tapes

____3. John Mitchell
c. White House counsel who refused to play the role of scapegoat and revealed the president's involvement in the cover-up

____4. G. Gordon Liddy
d. chair of the House Judiciary Committee, which conducted impeachment proceedings

____5. Archibald Cox
e. judge presiding over the trial of the Watergate burglars

f. White House "plumber" who plotted the Watergate break-in

COMPLETION

Answer the question or complete the statement by filling in the blanks with the correct word or words.

1. Four hundred thousand young people gathered in upstate New York in the late 1960s for the _____ concert, the climactic event of the decade's cultural revolution.

2. During his first term as president, Nixon allowed Vice President _____ to deliver scathing attacks against Democratic liberals and their allies in the media.

3. In February 1972, Nixon met with the communist leaders of _____, ending more than two decades of diplomatic isolation.

4. Student protest over Nixon's bombing of Cambodia in 1970 ended in tragedy at _____ when four students were killed by National Guardsmen breaking up a demonstration.

5. Running on a platform advocating a negotiated settlement in Vietnam, the right to abortion, and tolerance of diverse lifestyles, Democratic nominee for president in 1972 Senator _____ was perceived as too liberal by many American voters.

6. On October 6, 1973, Egypt and Syria launched a surprise attack on _____, hoping to recapture lands they had lost in the prior war of 1967.

7. High-technology industries expanded tremendously after development of the _____, a small microprocessor that sped complex calculations for computers.

8. During the Ford administration, a Senate committee headed by Frank Church of Idaho investigated the actions of the _____, a federal agency involved in plots to assassinate foreign leaders.

9. In mid-1979, dictator Anastasio Somoza of _____ capitulated to the Sandinistas, the leaders of a leftist regime which developed close ties with Castro's Cuba.

10. The Cold War resumed with full fury in December 1979 when the Soviet Union invaded _____, a move designed to ensure a regime friendly to the USSR.

TRUE/FALSE

Mark the following statements either T (True) or F (False).

_____1. Despite legislative gains by the mid-1960s, American blacks had actually fallen farther behind whites in disposable income since the beginning of the integration movement.

_____2. College activists took the lead in denouncing the Vietnam War because they were the most likely candidates among America's youth to be drafted and engaged in combat.

_____3. A specific provision prohibiting discrimination in employment on the basis of sex was first enacted in the Equal Rights Amendment of 1972.

_____4. Nixon won the election of 1968 by the smallest share of the popular vote of any winning candidate since 1916.

_____5. By nature, Nixon was a gregarious and personable president who preferred the limelight of domestic leadership to the tangled world of foreign affairs.

_____6. Despite Nixon's appointment of four rather conservative judges to the Supreme Court, the new Court rendered relatively liberal decisions concerning busing, abortion, wiretapping, and the death penalty.

_____7. The showdown between the federal government and the press over publication of the Pentagon papers contributed to the "siege mentality" of the Nixon administration.

_____8. Although a symbolic first step toward nuclear arms control, the United States Senate bitterly opposed the SALT I treaty because it allowed the Soviets a strategic advantage by recognizing their existing lead in numbers of missiles.

MULTIPLE CHOICE

Circle the one alternative that *best* completes the statement or answers the question.

1. The Students for a Democratic Society (SDS) was a student organization of the 1960s
    a. protesting poverty, racism, and violence in America.
    b. emphasizing group participation and control as its main tactic for social change.
    c. denouncing drugs, rock music, and liberated sex as signs of a degenerate culture.
    d. supporting American involvement in the Vietnam War.

2. In contrast to the position of women in American society in the 1920s, by 1960
   a. more women enrolled in college and professional studies.
   b. more women were working, but for wages less than those earned by similarly trained men.
   c. women tended to enter professional careers rather than traditionally female work roles.
   d. the advertising media abandoned stereotypical sex roles in depictions of husbands and wives.

3. The election of 1968 witnessed all of the following bizarre events *except* the
   a. assassination of a presidential contender.
   b. withdrawal from the race by an incumbent president.
   c. large scale boycott of the election by southern voters.
   d. emergence of the most successful third-party candidate in fifty years.

4. As president, Richard Nixon sought to
   a. overthrow the Great Society legislation of the Johnson years.
   b. streamline the federal bureaucracy in a search for efficiency.
   c. shift responsibility for social problems from state and local authorities to Washington.
   d. appoint more liberal judges to the Supreme Court.

5. The most successful tactic employed by Nixon in calming American protest as he sought an end to the Vietnam War was his
   a. renewed bombing of communist supply lines.
   b. hard-line negotiations with Hanoi.
   c. gradual withdrawal of American troops.
   d. order for the mining of Haiphong harbor.

6. The truce ending the Vietnam War did *not* require or allow which of the following provisions?
   a. the release of all American prisoners of war.
   b. U.S. removal of its troops from South Vietnam within sixty days.
   c. maintenance of North Vietnamese troops in South Vietnam.
   d. the removal of all communist troops from South Vietnam.

7. The Nixon administration sought to suppress the Pentagon Papers mainly because publication of the papers might
   a. detail how successive presidents had avoided war in Southeast Asia.
   b. force a dramatic showdown with the press over First Amendment rights.
   c. reveal many embarrassing mistakes by American policymakers.
   d. signal to foreign governments an inability of the United States to maintain security.

8. The most damaging evidence against Nixon in the impeachment proceedings was the
   a. existence of taped conversations implicating him in attempts to cover up details of the Watergate break-in.
   b. testimony of White House counsel John Dean revealing Nixon's personal involvement.
   c. record of orders by Nixon to use government agencies to "punish" his enemies.
   d. discovery of large and illegal campaign contributions made to the Committee to Re-Elect the President.

9. The Yom Kippur or October War of 1973
   a. lasted only six days, as Israeli military dominance prevailed over Arab aggression.
   b. resulted in Israeli seizure of the Golan Heights from Syria, the Sinai peninsula from Egypt, and Jerusalem and the West Bank from Jordan.
   c. led to American demands for a strong pro-Israeli peace settlement.
   d. led to the Arab oil embargo, imposed to pressure Israel to return Arab lands seized in 1967.

10. The rampant inflation of the 1970s was caused by all of the following factors *except* the
    a. heavy government expenditures on the Vietnam War.
    b. heavy tax increases imposed by the Carter administration.
    c. worldwide shortage of food.
    d. sixfold increase in petroleum prices.

11. President Gerald R. Ford gained public support and confidence with his
    a. full and unconditional pardon granted to Richard Nixon.
    b. defense of CIA involvement in assassination plots.
    c. determination to undermine Great Society programs.
    d. forceful response to the *Mayaguez* crisis.

12. Jimmy Carter attracted votes in the election of 1976 with his
    a. self-portrayal as a candid and honest "outsider" offering fresh leadership.
    b. forceful stands on the major issues.
    c. calculated appeals to the affluent, the well-educated, and conservative suburbanites.
    d. well-reasoned political philosophy and clear sense of direction.

13. Which of the following responses was taken by Carter toward Latin America?
    a. opposition to negotiation with Panama over control of the Canal Zone
    b. support for Nicaraguan leader Anastasio Somoza
    c. authorization of increased military aid to the government of El Salvador
    d. establishment of closer ties with Cuba

14. Militant Iranian students seized the United States embassy in Teheran and took fifty-eight American hostages to protest
    a. America's attempt to reestablish an Iranian government under the shah's control.
    b. the shah's entry into the United States for medical treatment.
    c. American diplomatic and economic sanctions levied against Iran.
    d. an American helicopter mission sent to overthrow the Khomeini regime.

15. The American policy of détente with the USSR was hampered in the late 1970s by
    a. Leonid Brezhnev's denunciations of American actions.
    b. Carter's advocacy of a new MX missile for the United States.
    c. America's refusal to allow the emigration of Soviet Jews.
    d. China's refusal to normalize relations with the United States.

THOUGHT QUESTIONS

To check your understanding of the key issues of this period, solve the following problems:

1. Why was the 1960s a decade of "cultural insurgency"? Discuss the various groups which engaged in protest as well as the purposes and results of such protests.

2. Account for the resurgence of the Republican party in the late 1960s and early 1970s.

3. The text argues that the Watergate episode "revealed both the weaknesses and strength of the American political system." Explain.

4. What caused the "energy crisis" of the 1970s? Discuss the political as well as economic consequences of the energy crises.

5. Discuss the successes and failures of the Carter administration in terms of foreign policy. What problems eroded the policy of détente and renewed a Cold War atmosphere during Carter's administration?

CHAPTER 32

THE REAGAN–BUSH ERA

SUMMARY
A charismatic politician who stressed themes of reduced government, balanced budgets, protection of family values, and peace through increased military spending, Reagan was the perfect candidate for the Republicans at a time of growing national conservatism.

THE CONSERVATIVE RESURGENCE: REAGAN IN POWER

The Reagan Victory
The failure of Carter's economic policies and America's weak image abroad were issues seized by Reagan in the 1980 campaign. Reagan scored important points in a televised debate and captured a decisive victory in the election. The Republicans also made major gains in the congressional elections, substantiating a thorough repudiation of Carter and his policies.

Cutting Spending and Taxes
Reagan supported supply-side economics, seeking to diminish the tax burden on the private sector and enhance investment-oriented growth. Reduction of government spending would hopefully ease inflation. Major congressional victories gave Reagan a 25 percent cut in personal income taxes over three years and significant reduction of domestic appropriations for social services.

Limiting the Role of Government
Under the direction of Reagan and cabinet officials such as Interior Secretary James Watt and Transportation Secretary Drew Lewis, deregulation of the economy and restriction of federal activities became a major theme. Congress attempted to slow the rapid growth of Social Security benefits with legislative changes in 1983. Feminist groups and minorities found Reagan's policies disappointing.

Reaganomics
After a temporary recession in 1981-1982 (which included as one casualty the supply-side theory), the economy rebounded in 1983 with the automobile industry, consumer spending, and low inflation fueling economic growth.

The Growing Deficit
The failure of supply-side economics fed a huge and growing federal deficit. Congress responded with the Gramm-Rudman Act, a compromise that forced the president to give up further increases in the defense budget while Democrats sacrificed hopes for expanded social programs. A decline in exports led to an alarming second deficit-in the balance of overseas trade. Foreign investment

turned the United States into a debtor nation in 1985. Reaganomics succeeded in continuing a high American standard of living only as a result of a massive borrowing which threatened the economic security of future generations.

The Politics of Prosperity
Under Reagan, the rich got richer, the middle class scrambled to hold its own, and the poor stayed poor. Nevertheless, Republicans convinced Americans that Reaganomics worked, enabling the president to easily defeat Democrats Walter Mondale and Geraldine Ferraro. Yet voters revealed mixed feelings by giving Democrats control of the House and gains in the Senate.

REAGAN AND THE WORLD
Determined to alter America's shattered image abroad, Reagan continued the hard line adopted toward Russia and the massive military buildup begun by Carter and approved of new offensive weapons systems.

Challenging the "Evil Empire"
Denouncing Soviet-sponsored terrorism and human rights violations, Reagan depicted the Soviet Union as the "evil empire" and pushed for the deployment of additional missiles in European NATO locations. Prompted by Soviet intransigence on arms control, the United States quickened the pace of Strategic Defense Initiative ("Star Wars") research and development. The arms race between the superpowers reached its most dangerous level ever.

Turmoil in the Middle East
The United States made no significant effort to halt the Israeli invasion of Lebanon in 1982, but did agree to send troops under multinational direction to Beirut to permit the evacuation of the Palestine Liberation Organization (PLO). The vulnerability of American noncombat troops was underscored by the destruction of a marine barracks in 1983, and the Arab-Israeli conflict continued to worsen.

Confrontation in Central America
In Nicaragua, the Sandinistas overthrew the Somoza regime in 1979. Although Carter had previously authorized economic aid for the Sandinistas, Reagan reversed that policy. Accusing the Sandinistas of accepting Cuban and Soviet military assistance, the president opted for covert support for the anti-government Contras. In El Salvador, the Reagan administration supported the moderate leader José Napoléon Duarte against left-wing guerrillas. American forces invaded the small Caribbean island of Grenada in October 1983 to confront Cuban workers and troops and prevent the communists from acquiring a strategic military base.

Trading Arms for Hostages
An initiative in 1985 aimed at improving American influence in the Middle East by establishing contact with moderates in Iran deteriorated into an arms for hostages deal. In 1986, members of the National Security Council staff tied this initiative to an illegal and unconstitutional scheme to funnel arms profits to the Contras in Nicaragua. Although Reagan was never personally tied to the diversion of funds, his popularity dropped rapidly.

Reagan the Peacemaker
The ascendancy of a more moderate Soviet leader in 1985, Mikhail Gorbachev, offered hope for improved U.S.-Soviet relations. With Reagan hoping to rebound from the Iran-Contra affair and Gorbachev anxious to repair the Soviet economy, the two world leaders held a series of meetings during Reagan's second term. As a result, a treaty was signed in late 1987 banning intermediate nuclear missiles. U.S.-Soviet cooperation eased tensions in a number of global hot spots, further enhancing Reagan's reputation.

PASSING THE TORCH

The Changing Palace Guard
Reagan used the interplay of his chief of staff, White House counsel, and special counsel to carefully guide his first administration. In 1985, however, these key advisors took different positions and achieved only limited success. Attorney General Edwin Meese led an assault on judicial activism, but soon encountered charges of unethical conduct. Critics noted a "sleaze factor" with assorted administration officials involved in various scandals. Coupled with the Iran-Contra affair, these scandals indicated that Reagan's tendency to delegate authority to subordinates had weakened his presidency.

The Election of 1988
Republican strategists effectively deflected public attention from such issues as the Iran-Contra affair and budget woes by portraying the Democratic candidate, Michael Dukakis, as soft on crime and defense. Although the Democrats increased their control in Congress, repeated promises by Republican candidate George Bush not to raise taxes-reminding voters of the economy's health-helped the GOP retain the White House.

Defaults and Deficits
The majority of Bush's time was taken by two pressing domestic problems: the cleanup of the nation's savings-and-loan industry and the challenge of stemming the ever-growing federal deficits. The latter problem forced Bush to break his promise of no new taxes and initiate substantial spending cuts, mainly for the military.

The End of the Cold War
An attempt at internal liberation by Chinese students proved tragically premature, while communist regimes in Eastern Europe collapsed with surprising speed in mid-1989 once it became apparent that Gorbachev would not use Soviet power to support them. By late 1991, both Gorbachev and the Soviet Union became victims of the demise of communism. Bush negotiated first with Gorbachev, then with Russian President Boris Yeltsin on the START I and II treaties, significantly reducing nuclear weapons on each side.

Waging Peace
The end of the Cold War did not mean a world free of violence. In December 1989, the United States invaded Panama to overthrow the regime of drug-trafficking General Manuel Noriega. In

January 1991, the United States began an aerial assault leading to a ground offensive the next month against Iraq, aiming to free Kuwait and protect the vital oil resources of the Persian Gulf.

DEMOCRATIC RESURGENCE

In the 1940s, historian Arthur M. Schlesinger, Sr., devised a theory of political cycles, noting alternating eras of reform and conservatism in American history. According to Schlesinger's predictions, the next wave of liberal activism is due in the 1990s.

The Election of 1992

A persistent recession became the primary focus of the 1992 campaign. Eccentric billionaire H. Ross Perot, running as an independent candidate, singled out the deficit as the nation's gravest problem. Democrat Bill Clinton championed economic renewal, stressing the need for investment in the nation's infrastructure and reform of job training and health care. While voters rejected Bush and elected Clinton, questions remained as to what specific changes the electorate wanted most.

LEARNING OBJECTIVES

After mastering the chapter, you should be able to

1. Discuss the reasons for a conservative resurgence and the election of Ronald Reagan in 1980.

2. Summarize the theory of supply-side economics and how it translated into specific legislation under Reagan.

3. Identify the legislative victories as well as the disappointments of Reagan's first-term domestic policy.

4. Discuss Reagan's first-term approach to the Soviet Union, the arms race, and options for the future.

5. Analyze the success of Reagan's foreign policies in the Middle East and Central America.

6. Explain the events of the Iran-Contra affair.

7. Analyze the motivations and results of Reagan's attempts at peacemaking during his second term.

8. Discuss the candidates, issues, and results of the election of 1988.

9. Explain the pressing domestic problems which preoccupied the Bush administration.

10. Discuss the reasons for and results of the Persian Gulf War in 1991.

11. Describe the series of events which signalled an end to the Cold War.

12. Account for the Democratic resurgence and victory in the election of 1992.

GLOSSARY

To build your social science vocabulary, familiarize yourself with the following terms:

1. **strident** harsh; shrill. "In contrast to Goldwater's strident rhetoric, Reagan used relaxed, confident, and persuasive terms. . . . "

2. **ideologue** an adherent of a particular set of ideas. ". . . without appearing to be a rigid ideologue of the right."

3. **think tanks** associated researchers who study and report on important questions of public policy. "Scholars and academics on the right flourished in new 'think tanks'. . . ."

4. **onus** burden or disagreeable obligation. ". . . leaving Carter with the onus of trying to land a low blow."

5. **vendetta** a vengeful retaliation or blood feud. "George McGovern and Frank Church met with defeat, victims of a vendetta waged by the Moral Majority."

6. **entitlement** a legal right to something; a stipend for which someone has worked or qualified. "Quickly deciding not to attack such popular middle-class entitlement programs as Social Security and Medicare."

7. **unilateral** one-sided; action by one country. "This unilateral Japanese action enabled the Reagan administration to help Detroit's car makers. . . ."

8. **solvency** a state of being able to pay all debts. "Congress finally approved a series of changes that guaranteed the solvency of Social Security."

9. **deployment** the act of placing into a battle-ready position a military unit or a piece of military hardware. "The Democrats . . . included plans for cruise missiles in Europe, a rapid deployment force in the Middle East. . . ."

10. **deterrence** the act or process of discouraging or preventing. ". . . the deadly trap of deterrence, with its reliance on the threat of nuclear retaliation to keep the peace."

11. **covert** hidden; secret. ". . . Reagan opted for covert action."

12. **charismatic** marked by strong personal appeal. "Reagan . . . as a detached but charismatic chief executive."

13. **impropriety** quality or state of being improper or unacceptable. " . . . some of Meese's dealings had the 'appearance' of impropriety."

14. **recriminations** bitter responses; retaliations. "Not only did Bush face recriminations from voters for breaking his 'read my lips' pledge. . . ."

15. **euphoric** marked by elation and joy. " . . . a sentiment widely shared by a euphoric public."

IDENTIFICATION

Briefly identify the meaning and significance of the following terms.

1. supply-side economics _____
_____

2. Sandra Day O'Connor _____
_____

3. Gramm-Rudman Act _____
_____

4. Oliver North _____
_____

5. Strategic Defense Initiative (SDI) _____
_____

6. Chernobyl _____
_____

7. Mikhail Gorbachev _____
_____

8. Michael Dukakis _____
_____

9. Tiananmen Square _____

_____

10. Saddam Hussein _____

_____

MATCHING

A. Match the following members of the Reagan administration with the appropriate description.

____ 1. James Watt

____ 2. Edwin Meese

____ 3. Drew Lewis

____ 4. Caspar Weinberger

____ 5. George Schultz

a. secretary of transportation who relieved the troubled American automobile industry by easing federal pollution and safety regulations

b. attorney general charged with unethical conduct

c. secretary of the treasury who questioned the wisdom of supply-side economics

d. secretary of state who strenuously objected to the policy of trading arms for hostages

e. secretary of defense who presented plans for more than a doubling of defense spending from 1981 to 1986

f. secretary of the interior who outraged environmentalists by opening federal lands to coal and timber production

B. Match each of the following countries with the appropriate description.

____ 1. Lebanon

____ 2. Israel

a. the Reagan administration opposed the government of this country by supplying its armed enemies with covert aid

b. the Reagan administration supported its moderate government under José Napoléon Duarte

____ 3. Grenada c. the Reagan administration tacitly supported its armed invasion of a neighboring country

____ 4. El Salvador d. the Reagan administration ordered the American marines to invade this country

____ 5. Nicaragua e. the Reagan administration ordered the withdrawal of American forces from this country after a terrorist attack killed 239 marines

f. the Reagan administration supported this embattled democracy with covert action against its several totalitarian neighbors

COMPLETION

Answer the question or complete the statement by filling in the blanks with the correct word or words.

1. Radio and television evangelist Jerry Falwell founded the _____, a fundamentalist group intent on preserving and promoting conservative values.

2. Walter Mondale became the first presidential candidate of a major political party to choose a woman as his running mate when he selected New York Congresswoman _____ as the Democratic vice presidential nominee in 1984.

3. An accident at the nuclear power plant at _____ in the United States left a legacy of fear that has eroded popular support for nuclear power.

4. In 1984, Congress prohibited any United States agency from spending money in Central America with passage of the _____.

5. Gorbachev was intent upon improving Soviet relations with the United States as a part of his new policies of _____ (restructuring the Soviet economy) and _____ (political openness).

6. The Senate rejected Reagan's nomination for a Supreme Court Justice position for _____, an outspoken critic of judicial activism.

7. In June 1989, Lech Walesa and his Solidarity movement came to power in free elections in _____.

8. Newly-elected President of the Russian Republic, _____ helped break up a military coup and secure the release of Gorbachev from right-wing plotters.

9. In December 1989, the United States invaded Panama to overthrow the government of drug-trafficking General _____.

10. An independent candidate for president in 1992, _____ argued that the deficit represented the nation's gravest problem.

MULTIPLE CHOICE

Circle the one alternative that *best* completes the statement or answers the question.

1. As Governor of California, Ronald Reagan
   a. proved effective, but rigid in supporting only conservative measures.
   b. confronted campus radicals and slashed funds for higher education.
   c. emerged as a masterful politician, especially adept in scoring symbolic victories.
   d. all of the above

2. The conservative resurgence of the late 1970s and early 1980s resulted from an increasing
   a. public frustration with liberal reliance on government to solve the nation's problems.
   b. concern about greater social and sexual permissiveness in American society.
   c. fear that liberals had been too soft on the communist threat abroad.
   d. all of the above

3. According to the theories of supply-side economics, embraced by Reagan as the solution to the nation's economic ills,
   a. the federal government should increase spending to boost consumer demand.
   b. federal spending as well as taxes should be cut to release private revenue for productive investments.
   c. taxes should be increased and spending decreased by the federal government to help eliminate the budget deficit.
   d. funding for entitlement programs should be increased to pump more money into the economy.

4. Among Reagan's most significant political successes in domestic affairs were his
   a. budgetary and tax reforms.
   b. increased governmental restrictions in land and resource development.
   c. overhauls of the Social Security System.
   d. advancement of civil rights and women's rights.

5. American marines were sent to Lebanon in 1982 to
   a. help Israel secure its northern border.
   b. aid the Christian faction in its war against Moslem forces.
   c. join a multinational peacekeeping force during the evacuation of the PLO.
   d. avenge the terrorist truck-bombing of an American barracks.

6. The policy of the Reagan administration to trade arms for hostages was "fatally flawed" in that it
   a. contradicted the spirit of the Boland Amendment.
   b. failed to win compliance from the Iranians.
   c. led to the seizure of additional American prisoners.
   d. encouraged an end to the war between Iran and Iraq.

7. When Congress seemed reluctant to seek a military solution to America's troubled relations with the Sandinistas, the Reagan administration supported instead
   a. covert action by the CIA in support of the Contras.
   b. economic assistance to moderate the Sandinista coalition.
   c. solutions of land reform and redistribution of wealth.
   d. negotiations initiated by countries of Central and South America.

8. Which of the following best explains the 1981-1982 recession?
   a. Reagan's insistence on a massive military buildup
   b. the tight money policy of the Federal Reserve Board
   c. sharp reductions in personal income taxes
   d. the dramatic reduction of government spending for social services

9. The major problem accompanying the economic expansion of the 1980s was a(n)
   a. increase in the cost of living.
   b. reduction in consumer spending.
   c. significant decline in the Dow Jones industrial average.
   d. mounting federal deficit.

10. Soviet leader Mikhail Gorbachev supported the
    a. adoption of a socialist economy for the Soviet Union.
    b. supply of Mujadeen guerrillas fighting in Afghanistan.
    c. limitation of political parties within the Soviet Union.
    d. removal of Soviet forces propping up repressive regimes in Eastern Europe.

11. In his relations with the Supreme Court, Ronald Reagan
    a. refused to consider the appointment of a female justice.
    b. appointed conservative William Rehnquist as chief justice.
    c. supported a policy of judicial activism.
    d. tried to balance the court with liberal as well as conservative appointees.

12. The summit meetings between Reagan and Gorbachev led to an agreement in 1987 to
    a. abolish all nuclear weapons in a decade.
    b. ban all intermediate nuclear weapons.
    c. abandon plans for any "star wars" projects.
    d. reduce conventional forces around the world.

13. During the campaign of 1988, George Bush
    a. portrayed Dukakis as soft on crime and defense.
    b. hinted that mounting federal deficits might require tax increases.
    c. disassociated himself from the Reagan administration.
    d. called for meaningful health care reform.

14. From 1989 to 1991, communist regimes collapsed in all of the following countries *except*
    a. Poland.
    b. East Germany.
    c. China.
    d. the Soviet Union.

15. According to the theory of American political cycles advanced by historian Arthur M. Schlesinger, Sr., the 1990s in the United States is likely to be a time of
    a. conservative consolidation.
    b. liberal activism.
    c. isolationism and retrenchment.
    d. opportunism and graft.

THOUGHT QUESTIONS

To check your understanding of the key issues of the period, solve the following problems:

1. Did Reagan's victory in 1980 signal a major realignment in American politics with the Republicans becoming the majority party?

2. Analyze the success of the Reagan administration in curing the nation's economic woes.

3. Reagan began his administration by characterizing the Soviet Union as a deadly enemy and the "evil empire." By the end of his presidency, however, he had assumed the role of peacemaker and pointed to the end of the Cold War. Trace the evolution of events which allowed this change.

4. The deal to trade United States arms to Iran for hostages was bad policy, but the Iran-Contra affair was criminal. Explain.

5. Discuss the events which signalled an end to the Cold War during the Bush administration.

6. In what ways did "Desert Storm" bring mixed blessings to the Bush administration? Why did Bush lose the election of 1992?

CHAPTER 33

AMERICA IN FLUX, 1970–1993

THE CHANGING AMERICAN POPULATION

A People on the Move
The 1970s and 1980s found the American population moving to the "Sunbelt" states of the South and West-although that shift had begun to slow somewhat-while growing increasingly urban and older.

The Revival of Immigration
The pace of immigration rose steadily, by 1992 reaching a million a year, matching the record level of the years 1900 to 1910. The new immigrants came largely from Asia and Latin America, increasing considerably the number of U.S. foreign-born and ethnic-minority Americans.

Advance and Retreat for African Americans
Many African Americans gained better education and employment in the 1970s and 1980s; many joined the movement to the Sunbelt and integrated the South more thoroughly than any other section of the country. Affirmative action, legislation, and court decisions yielded mixed results; median income remained low and unemployment high. Those without education suffered extremely high unemployment, especially during the recession of 1990-91. Many young urban African Americans could look forward to little more than staying alive. A few expressed their frustration in the riots which followed the not guilty verdict for the Los Angeles police officers accused in the beating of Rodney King.

The Emerging Hispanics
Hispanic Americans constituted the second largest minority, their numbers growing rapidly to reach 23 million in 1990, including the "undocumented aliens" who stirred a national debate over their supposed economic dangers or benefits to the country. On the whole, young, poor and under-educated, their economic gains in the boom of the 1980s raised their median family income, but only to 66 percent of the level of other Americans. In spite of a 1986 law designed to address the problem of illegal Hispanic immigration, a new surge of illegal entrants began in the early 1990s. Already providing enough voters to become a significant force in American politics, Hispanics were projected to become the nation's largest minority by 2010.

Asian Americans on the March
In the 1980s Asians provided 46 percent of immigration to America and constituted the highest percentage of foreign born of any ethnic group. Here, with the partial exception of refugees from Southeast Asia, they have made remarkable progress on "the mountain of gold," prospering as the "most upwardly mobile group in the country."

Melting Pot or Multiethnic Diversity
The analogy of the melting pot, always dubious, seemed irrelevant to America's growing ethnic diversity of the 1980s; from controversial educational curriculum to uncertain personal identity, cultural pluralism challenged the country to confront the dilemma of *E Pluribus Unum*, to balance ethnic pride with national unity.

PRIVATE LIVES--PUBLIC ISSUES
In the last two decades American private lives emerged as public issues as women and homosexuals demanded an end to discrimination.

The Changing American Family
In spite of campaign references to family values, social changes assailed traditional family life; more Americans postponed or abandoned marriage, more women worked outside the home,and the number of people living alone increased markedly. By 1990,25 percent of the nation's children lived in one-parent families, usually with a mother, and too often in poverty.

Gains and Setbacks for Women
Increasing numbers of the country's women entered the workforce, and did so for an average of only 72 percent of men's pay. They made some gains in professional employment and political offices, but usually worked in female-dominated fields, and soon struck a "glass ceiling" in male-dominated fields. The women's movement failed to gain ratification of the Equal Rights Amendment and struggled to protect its hard-won right to abortion.

The Gay Liberation Movement
The Stonewall riots of 1969 initiated an organized liberation movement for American gays to "come out of the closet," to combat discrimination and to affirm pride in their sexual preference. In the 1980s they redirected much of the struggle for gay rights to focus on the effects of the AIDS epidemic; ACT UP began a series of violent demonstrations for greater public funding to conquer the disease. By the 1990s gays and lesbians had forced recognition of their rights. Yet the intense resistance to President Clinton's attempt to end the ban on gays in the military revealed mainstream reluctance to accept homosexuality.

SOCIAL DILEMMAS
Two serious social problems came to the public awareness in the 1980s, but neither was addressed quickly or adequately by the Reagan and Bush administrations.

The AIDS Epidemic
During the 1980s,a mysterious and deadly disease known as AIDS (acquired immune deficiency syndrome) developed into a major public health issue. The Reagan administration was slow to respond to the threat with a weak and inconsistent commitment to research, public information, and care. By the early 1990s, he "gay disease" seemed destined to grow far beyond any one group, to become the most deadly disease in American history.

The War on Drugs
The use of cocaine, especially the cheaper derivative known as "crack," threatened the peace and security of the inner city. By the end of the decade the public regarded drug abuse as society's most serious problem. Neither the Reagan nor Bush efforts at interdiction proved successful. Clinton shifted that effort to an attempt to reduce demand through treatment of addicts.

ECONOMIC DILEMMAS
For over two decades economic strains-recession, unemployment, stagnant family income, structural changes and Reagan tax policies-eroded American confidence in the economy.

The Rich Grow Richer
In the 1980s American white-collar employment grew at the expense of blue-collar workers and the rich gained considerably in both income and wealth, a disparity resulting from: structural changes in the economy, a shift from well paid work in manufacturing to poorly paid service jobs, and Republican tax policies. Middle-class families paid more taxes for every dollar earned than the wealthy paid for each dollar of income.

Recession and Stagnation
In 1990 a recession followed economic inequities to devastate the Bush administration. Especially difficult for white-collar workers and the boom areas of the previous decade, the downturn proved particularly persistent when the end of the Cold War led to layoffs in the defense industry and German and Japanese economic booms put the U.S. in a difficult position in foreign trade. Disenchanted voters brought an end to the Reagan-Bush years.

The Plight of the Middle Class
Bill Clinton won the presidency by charging that Republicans had favored the rich at the expense of those average Americans whose median family income had remained stagnant for 20 years. Yet the middle class had shrunk not just because many in its ranks had fallen to a lower income group; many others had advanced to a wealthier level. But feelings of diminished expectations persisted, while most of the world envied our living standards.

LEARNING OBJECTIVES

After mastering this chapter, you should be able to

1. Summarize the reasons for the significant shifts or migrations of the American population in the seventies and eighties.

2. Outline the new trends and resulting effects of the "new immigration."

3. Identify the sources of economic improvement for African Americans as well as continued problems they faced.

4. Discuss the problems and grievances articulated by Hispanic Americans in recent history.

5. Explain the successes, challenges, and controversies of cultural awareness and diversity.

6. Identify the ways in which family life in America changed in the seventies and eighties.

7. Define the goals and challenges facing the recent women's movement.

8. Summarize the factors and considerations which drove the gay liberation movement.

9. Analyze the severity of the AIDS threat to American society and the controversies associated with combating it.

10. Identify the reasons why illegal drug use became a national crisis in the eighties.

11. List and explain the factors contributing to the growing income disparity in the 1980s.

12. Evaluate the reasons for the decline in expectations of the American middle class.

13. Outline the limitless possibilities in our national culture for the future.

GLOSSARY

To build your social science vocabulary, familiarize yourself with the following terms:

1. **affirmative action** policies designed to promote the interests of minority applicants to help compensate for past discrimination. "Dismissing affirmative action as 'social engineering' . . ."

2. **sexual harassment** persistent, unwanted sexual remarks, looks or advances directed toward a subordinate or co-worker, causing him or her to feel demeaned or intimidated. "The question of sexual harassment, a traditional feminist grievance, took on new importance."

3. **Sunbelt** referring to the geographic area of the southern states, mainly from Texas to Florida. "The Sunbelt, best defined as a broad band running across the country below the thirty-seventh parallel. . . ."

4. **racial quotas** to base hiring, appointment, or promotion on strict numerical percentages of minorities as part of affirmative action. ". . . the Court ruled against such rigid racial quotas."

5. **corporate downsizing** the policy of companies to diminish output or employment due to business considerations. "Individual companies denied any racial motivation, attributing the job cuts to 'corporate downsizing.'"

6. **undocumented aliens** people who enter the country illegally for the purpose of residing there. "The entry of several million illegal immigrants from Mexico, once derisively called 'wetbacks' and now known as 'undocumented aliens'. . . ."

7. **ethnic diversity** the condition of a population group having cultural and racial differences. "The new awareness of ethnic diversity manifested itself in many ways."

8. **Eurocentric** predominate emphasis on European cultural, historical, or ethnic importance or contribution. "In public education, blacks led a crusade against Eurocentric curriculum. . . ."

9. **right-to-life** individuals or groups who favor the elimination or outlawing of all abortions. "Right-to-life groups, consisting mainly of orthodox Catholics, fundamentalist Protestants, and conservatives. . . ."

10. **gay liberation** promotion of the rights and considerations of homosexuals. "The basic theme of gay liberation was to urge all homosexuals to come out of the closet. . . ."

11. **AIDS** acquired immune deficiency syndrome; a viral epidemic usually transmitted by sexual contact or the use of intravenous drug needles. "The outbreak of AIDS (acquired immune deficiency syndrome) in the early 1980s took most Americans by surprise."

12. **interdiction** the act of prohibiting or stopping before the fact. "In the mid-1980s, the administration began to place greater emphasis on interdiction. . . ."

13. **economic restructuring** policies or activities which change the economic nature or infrastructure. "The income disparity was the product of both economic restructuring and Republican tax policy."

14. **gross domestic product** the annual sum of all goods and services produced in the U.S. "For the next eight months, the gross domestic product (GDP) fell by 2.2 percent. . . ."

15. **global economy** the economic output and activity of all nations in trade or competition. ". . . while masking a growing lack of competitiveness in the global economy."

IDENTIFICATION

Briefly identify the meaning and significance of the following terms.

1. *Bakke* decision _____

_____

2. Chicanos _____

_____

3. Equal Rights Amendment _____

_____

4. National Organization for Women _____

_____

5. *Roe v. Wade* _____

_____

6. Hyde amendment _____

_____

7. ACT UP _____

_____

8. War on Drugs _____

_____

9. Drug Enforcement Agency _____

_____

10. C. Everett Koop _____

_____

MATCHING

A. Match the following women with the appropriate description.

_____ 1. Anita Hill   **a.** with "just say no" chose drug education as addition to War on Drugs

_____ 2. Sandra Day O'Connor   **b.** led efforts by conservatives to defeat the ERA

____3. Phyllis Schlafly   c. accused Supreme Court nominee of sexual harassment

____4. Nancy Reagan   d. appointed by President Reagan as first woman on the Supreme Court

____5. Ruth Bader Ginsberg   e. first female astronaut in outer space

                                     f. pro choice selection of President Clinton for Supreme Court

B. Match each of the following men with the appropriate description.

____1. Clarence Thomas   a. first African American governor of a southern state since Reconstruction

____2. Rodney King   b. Georgia Senator who opposed President Clinton's proposal to end ban on gays in the military

____3. Henry Cisneros   c. San Antonio mayor and HUD secretary under President Clinton

____4. Sam Nunn   d. his beating became a national symbols of African American frustration and of police brutality

____5. L. Douglas Wilder   e. conservative Supreme Court appointee who believed in "black self help"

                                     f. celebrity whose death due to cocaine overdose drew national attention to drug abuse

COMPLETION

Answer the question or complete the statement by filling in the blanks with the correct word or words.

1. Ronald Reagan appointed _____ as the first woman justice of the Supreme Court.

2. Right wing activist, _____ led an organized effort to defeat the ERA.

3. The issue of growing concern, _____, dominated the Judiciary Committee's hearings of Clarence Thomas and Anita Hill.

4. The area of the southern U.S. known as the _____ flourished with with rapid population growth in the seventies and eighties.

5. The new wave of immigrants during and after the 1960s came mainly from _____ and _____.

6. The key factor in preventing more economic progress for Hispanics in America was _____.

7. The _____ image was traditionally seen as stripping immigrants of their previous culture and casting them into an Anglo-Saxon mold.

8. The Supreme Court decision in 1972 which ruled that state laws restricting a woman's right to abortion were unconstitutional was _____.

9. The basic theme of _____ was to urge homosexuals to affirm their sexual identity with pride.

10. A Gallup poll taken in 1989 revealed that _____ had become the greatest concern of the American people.

TRUE/FALSE

Mark the following statements either T (True) or F (False).

_____1. During the 1970s, the numbers and political influence of elderly Americans increasingly declined.

_____2. Through the 1970s, African Americans continued to migrate northward and westward, fleeing prejudice and discrimination in the southern states.

_____3. Hispanics, people with Spanish surnames, represented the fastest growing ethnic group in the United States in the 1970s and 1980s.

_____4. President Reagan developed a quick and effective public education campaign in response to the AIDS threat.

_____5. In the 1980s, as a result of racism and global warming, the American people migrated to the North and East.

_____6. Asian Americans were successful compared to other ethnic groups.

_____7. As a result of the Equal Rights Amendment the pay of women equalled or surpassed that of men.

_____8. President Clinton altered the tactics of the war on drugs by emphasizing treatment for addicts.

_____9. The tax policies of the Reagan years resulted in shifting the burden from the middle class to the wealthy.

_____10. From 1970 to 1990 the emphasis by politicians on family values reduced the number of one-parent families.

MULTIPLE CHOICE

Circle the one alternative that *best* completes the statement or answers the question.

1. Defenders of illegal aliens who argued in favor of amnesty and against deportation pointed out that "illegals" had
   a. accepted low-paying and menial jobs usually shunned by most Americans.
   b. paid sales and withholding taxes but rarely used welfare services for fear of detection by government authorities.
   c. benefitted employers by providing laborers to whom they did not have to pay minimum wages, pensions, or other fringe benefits.
   d. all of the above

2. Between 1970 and 1980, Asian Americans
   a. earned educational and economic achievement disproportionate to their numbers.
   b. increased in numbers to comprise 10.5 percent of the total population.
   c. rejected traditional ethnic values in an effort to "Americanize" themselves.
   d. suffered increasing discrimination and ostracism in American society.

3. In the decades of the 1970s and 1980s, the population of the United States tended to
   a. migrate to a limited extent, but always remaining essentially close to family and friends.
   b. move to the "Sunbelt" states of the South and West.
   c. move to areas known for high social services and progressive political values.
   d. move to the previously lower populated North-Central states.

4. The population shifts of the 1970s and 1980s resulted in
   a. increased urbanization, greater ethnic diversity, and increased social unrest.
   b. increased rural population, greater ethnic homogeneity, and social stability.
   c. increased urbanization, greater ethnic homogeniety, and social unrest.
   d. increased rural population, greater ethnic diversity, and social unrest.

5. The analogy of the "melting pot"
   a. was true of the immigration of the early 1900s, but not possible for the more recent influx of immigrants.
   b. remained the stated goal of the nation throughout the twentieth century.
   c. was hardly a reality for the immigrants of eighty years ago and irrelevant to those involved in the recent immigration.
   d. was adopted by college faculty as the defining principle for the higher education curriculum.

6. Between 1970 and 1980 the American family
   a. increased in stability so that less than 10 percent of those in poverty were children.
   b. increased in strength because Republican candidates spoke so often on issues of family values in campaigns.
   c. was weakened because equal pay for women enticed many mothers to enter the workforce.
   d. underwent great stress resulting from social change.

7. From 1970 to 1990 American women
   a. increasingly entered the world of work.
   b. achieved equal pay for equal work.
   c. left female-dominated fields.
   d. reduced the number of working women.

8. The gay liberation movement of the 1970s and 1980s
   a. was diverted from its original goals because of its efforts to care for AIDS patients.
   b. succeeded in its goal to end the ban on gays in the military.
   c. failed to end the ban on gays in the military, but won support from mainstream America.
   d. was not always sucessful, but at least united all gays in support of the "coming out" strategy.

9. Acquired Immune Deficiency Syndrome (AIDS)
   a. was immediately seen as a threat to the general public.
   b. posed no threat to the general public outside of gay men and intravenous drug users.
   c. caused President Reagan's commission to criticize his slow and inconsistent response.
   d. was not a threat to the nation's blood supply.

10. As the Reagan administration addressed the problems of the 1980s, it
    a. followed a pro-California or pro-West strategy.
    b. was hampered by the desire to reduce the deficit.
    c. attacked drugs, AIDS, and immigration with equal vigor.
    d. was aggressive on AIDS and drugs but not on immigration.

11. One result of economic restructuring and Reagan tax policies was
    a. a stronger position for lower and middle income families.
    b. the growth of one-income families.
    c. absolute equal tax rates for all.
    d. the rich grew richer in both income and wealth.

12. The recession of 1990
    a. convinced the American people of the wisdom of Republican policies.
    b. led Americans to blame Congress but not the president.
    c. had a negative impact on the Bush administration.
    d. ended with the end of the Cold War.

13. Which of the following was not evidence of the decline of the midddle class?
    a. Median family income actually declined slightly from 1973 to 1992.
    b. Working wives became a necessity to maintain a decent standard of living.
    c. The percent of the population that was considered middle class declined from 71.2 percent in 1969 to 63.3 percent in 1989.
    d. Disposable income increased from $11,013 in 1973 to $14,154 in 1990.

14. The conflict between Clarence Thomas and Anita Hill
    a. was overwhelmingly decided in the Senate in favor of Clarence Thomas.
    b. raised issues of affirmative action and sexual harassment.
    c. was decided in the Judiciary Committee by the swing vote of women senators.
    d. was decided by way of Anita Hill's successfully passing a lie detector test.

15. Compared to the general population, Hispanic Americans were, on the whole
    a. older and better educated.
    b. younger, less educated, and poorer.
    c. more educated, but poorer.
    d. younger, but better educated.

THOUGHT QUESTIONS

To check your understanding of the key issues of the period, solve the following problems:

1. Do "illegals" contribute more to American society than they take from it? Support your position.

2. Is the concept of affirmative action fair? Why or why not?

3. Which shifts in the American economy and population during the 1970s and 1980s were likely to continue and why?

4. Why did the Equal Rights Amendment fail to gain ratification? Is it unnecessary?

5. How and why has public policy shifted on the abortion issue since the early 1970s?

6. Should the national government protect equal rights for gays and lesbians? Support your position.

7. Will the percentage of "traditional" American families increase in the next two decades? Why or why not?

8. Why do Asian immigrants to the U.S. prove so adept at "climbing the mountain of gold"?

9. Will the incidence of AIDS increase in the next two decades? If so, why and among what groups in American society? If not, why not?

ANSWER KEY

CHAPTER 16

Matching A
1. c
2. a
3. d
4. e
5. b

Matching B
1. c
2. e
3. c
4. b
5. d

Completion
1. Birth of a Nation
2. Thirteenth Amendment
3. pocket veto
4. investment capital
5. Fourteenth
6. sharecropper
7. greenbacks
8. Ku Klux Klan
9. businessmen, poor white farmers, blacks
10. spoilsmen

True/False
1. True
2. False
3. False
4. True
5. False
6. True
7. False
8. True
9. True
10. False

Multiple Choice
1. d
2. a
3. a
4. d
5. d
6. b
7. c
8. b
9. a
10. a
11. a
12. c
13. c
14. b
15. d

CHAPTER 17

Matching A
1. b
2. a
3. c
4. d
5. e

Matching B
1. c
2. d
3. e
4. f
5. b

Completion
1. land, water, timber
2. Wovoka
3. buffalo
4. Cody
5. Missouri
6. bureaus, immigration
7. McCoy

8. placer mining
9. dry farming
10. Hatch

True/False
1. F
2. F
3. F
4. T
5. T
6. F
7. T
8. F
9. T
10. T

Multiple Choice
1. d
2. c
3. a
4. c
5. d
6. a
7. d
8. d
9. c
10. c
11. c
12. b
13. b
14. d
15. a

CHAPTER 18

Matching A
1. b
2. f
3. e
4. a
5. c

Matching B
1. d
2. a
3. b
4. c
5. f

Completion
1. Corliss engine
2. Walt Whitman
3. American Railway Association
4. watered
5. J. P. Morgan
6. trust
7. two thousand, twenty-one thousand
8. $50, $500
9. mail-order
10. $7

True/False
1. T
2. F
3. F
4. F
5. F
6. T
7. T
8. T
9. F
10. F

Multiple Choice
1. b
2. c
3. a
4. d
5. c
6. c
7. d
8. c
9. b
10. b

11. d
12. c
13. d
14. a
15. a

CHAPTER 19

Matching A
1. b
2. e
3. c
4. a
5. f

Matching B
1. d
2. b
3. a
4. c
5. f

Completion
1. Dwight Moody
2. Mugwumps
3. Comstock
4. croquet
5. ragtime
6. *McGuffey's Reader*
7. nine, 15
8. Louis H. Sullivan
9. William M. Tweed

True/False
1. False
2. False
3. True
4. True
5. False
6. True
7. False
8. False
9. True
10. False

Multiple Choice
1. d
2. c
3. b
4. d
5. a
6. d
7. c
8. b
9. d
10. d
11. a
12. c
13. b
14. a
15. b

CHAPTER 20

Matching A
1. d
2. a
3. e
4. f
5. b

Matching B
1. c
2. e
3. f
4. a
5. b

Completion
1. Thomas Reed
2. Pendleton
3. subtreasury system
4. government jobs
5. 79 percent

6. Interstate Commerce Commission
7. James Weaver
8. Mark Hanna
9. *Coin's Financial School*
10. Dingley

True/False
1. True
2. False
3. True
4. False
5. False
6. False
7. False
8. True
9. True
10. True

Multiple Choice
1. d
2. a
3. b
4. a
5. b
6. c
7. a
8. b
9. a
10. c
11. c
12. a
13. a
14. d
15. c

CHAPTER 21

Matching A
1. c
2. f
3. b
4. e
5. a

Matching B
1. b
2. f
3. e
4. c
5. a

Completion
1. Rough Riders
2. Charles Darwin
3. Josiah Strong
4. Hawaii
5. Samoan
6. Benjamin F. Tracy
7. William Randolph, Joseph Pulitzer
8. George Dewey
9. Andrew Carnegie
10. Dr. Walter Reed

True/False
1. T
2. F
3. T
4. T
5. F
6. F
7. F
8. F
9. T
10. T

Multiple Choice
1. c
2. d
3. c
4. b
5. d
6. c
7. d

8. b
9. c
10. d
11. a
12. d
13. b
14. a
15. d

CHAPTER 22

Matching A
1. b
2. d
3. a
4. c
5. f

Matching B
1. b
2. d
3. e
4. a
5. c

Completion
1. Theodore Roosevelt
2. Federal Aid Roads
3. General Electric
4. hookworm
5. W. E. B. Du Bois
6. *padroni*
7. literacy test
8. Industrial Workers of the World (IWW)
9. jazz
10. Ashcan School

True/False
1. T
2. F
3. F
4. F
5. T
6. T
7. T
8. F
9. T
10. F

Multiple Choice
1. d
2. b
3. d
4. d
5. c
6. c
7. a
8. b
9. b
10. d
11. c
12. b
13. c
14. a
15. b

CHAPTER 23

Matching A
1. c
2. d
3. b
4. e
5. a

Matching B
1. e
2. f
3. c
4. b
5. d

Completion
1. "bully pulpit"
2. Commerce and Labor

3. The Hepburn Act
4. Payne-Aldrich Act
5. New Nationalism
6. Underwood Tariff Act
7. meat packing industry
8. limited working hours
9. free
10. optimism

True/False
1. True
2. False
3. False
4. True
5. False
6. True
7. False
8. False
9. True
10. True

Multiple Choice
1. a
2. a
3. d
4. c
5. b
6. a
7. c
8. a
9. b
10. c
11. a
12. d
13. c
14. b
15. a

CHAPTER 24

Matching A
1. d
2. e
3. a
4. b
5. c

Matching B
1. e
2. f
3. c
4. b
5. a

Completion
1. William Jennings Bryan
2. an isthmian canal
3. Root-Takahira Agreement
4. moral diplomacy
5. Porfirio Diaz
6. neutrality
7. submarine
8. peace or preparedness
9. Huerta
10. "New Negro"

True/False
1. False
2. True
3. False
4. False
5. True
6. False
7. False
8. False
9. True
10. False

Multiple Choice
1. c
2. b
3. a
4. d
5. a
6. d
7. c
8. a

9. c
10. a
11. a
12. b
13. b
14. a
15. c

CHAPTER 25

Matching A
1. c
2. d
3. f
4. e
5. b

Matching B
1. d
2. a
3. b
4. f
5. c

Completion
1. Model T
2. Samuel Insull
3. Equal Rights Amendment
4. Charles Lindbergh
5. W. E. B. Du Bois
6. Harlem Renaissance
7. A. Mitchell Palmer
8. Clarence Darrow
9. Albert Fall
10. Al Smith

True/False
1. F
2. F
3. F
4. T
5. T
6. T

7. F
8. F
9. T
10. F

Multiple Choice
1. c
2. c
3. a
4. d
5. a
6. c
7. c
8. b
9. c
10. a
11. b
12. a
13. a
14. c
15. c

CHAPTER 26

Matching A
1. c
2. e
3. f
4. b
5. a

Matching B
1. d
2. f
3. e
4. a
5. b

Completion
1. Boulder Dam
2. General Douglas McArthur
3. labor

4. National Recovery Administration
5. Henry A. Wallace
6. Father Charles Coughlin
7. Wagner Act
8. Rural Electrification Act
9. Congress of Industrial Organizations
10. Burton Wheeler

True/False
1. False
2. False
3. True
4. True
5. False
6. False
7. False
8. True
9. True
10. False

Multiple Choice
1. c
2. a
3. b
4. a
5. b
6. d
7. b
8. d
9. c
10. b
11. d
12. c
13. d
14. c
15. c

CHAPTER 27

Matching A
1. b
2. d
3. e
4. f
5. c

Matching B
1. c
2. f
3. a
4. e
5. d

Completion
1. Kellogg-Briand Treaty
2. Clark Memorandum
3. Five Power Treaty
4. Nazi-Soviet Pact
5. Wendell Willkie
6. General Erwin Rommel
7. Admiral Chester Nimitz
8. Harry Truman
9. Potsdam
10. Henry Stimson

True/False
1. F
2. T
3. T
4. T
5. F
6. F
7. T
8. F
9. T
10. F

Multiple Choice
1. b
2. a
3. d

4. c
5. a
6. b
7. a
8. b
9. c
10. a
11. d
12. a
13. b
14. b
15. d

CHAPTER 28

Matching A
1. e
2. c
3. d
4. f
5. b

Matching B
1. e
2. a
3. b
4. c
5. d

Completion
1. Germany
2. Greece, Turkey
3. loans, lend-lease
4. Chiang Kai-shek
5. collective security
6. multiple untruth
7. House Un-American Activities Committee
8. Whittaker Chambers
9. Dixicrats
10. Taft-Hartley

True/False
1. False
2. True
3. False
4. True
5. True
6. False
7. True
8. False
9. True
10. False

Multiple Choice
1. b
2. a
3. d
4. d
5. b
6. b
7. b
8. a
9. d
10. c
11. a
12. d
13. b
14. b
15. a

CHAPTER 29

Matching A
1. d
2. c
3. a
4. f
5. b

Matching B
1. b
2. c
3. e
4. d
5. a

Completion
1. suburbs
2. National Aeronautics and Space Administration
3. armed forces
4. moderation
5. nonviolence
6. interstate highway system
7. John Birch Society
8. passive resistance
9. segregation

True/False
1. False
2. True
3. False
4. False
5. False
6. True
7. False
8. True
9. True
10. False

Multiple Choice
1. c
2. a
3. c
4. c
5. a
6. d
7. b
8. a
9. c
10. a
11. d
12. c
13. a
14. d
15. d

CHAPTER 30

Matching A
1. b
2. e
3. d
4. f
5. c

Matching B
1. a
2. c
3. e
4. d
5. f

Completion
1. U-2
2. Lebanon
3. Sputnik
4. "the best and brightest"
5. flexible responsse
6. Alliance for Progress
7. Viet Cong
8. "hot line"
9. *The Arrogance of Power*
10. Great Society

True/False
1. True
2. False
3. True
4. True
5. False
6. True
7. False
8. False
9. True
10. False

Multiple Choice
1. b
2. b
3. a
4. c
5. b
6. d
7. c
8. a
9. d
10. b
11. a
12. d
13. a
14. b
15. a

CHAPTER 31

Match A
1. a
2. e
3. d
4. f
5. b

Match B
1. e
2. c
3. a
4. f
5. b

Completion
1. Woodstock
2. Spiro Agnew
3. China
4. Kent State University
5. George McGovern
6. Israel
7. silicon chip
8. CIA
9. Nicaragua
10. Afghanistan

True/False
1. T
2. F
3. F
4. T
5. F
6. T
7. T
8. F

Multiple Choice
1. a
2. b
3. c
4. b
5. c
6. d
7. d
8. a
9. d
10. b
11. d
12. a
13. c
14. b
15. b

CHAPTER 32

Matching A
1. f
2. b
3. a
4. e
5. d

Matching B
1. e
2. c
3. d
4. b
5. a

Completion
1. Moral Majority
2. Geraldine Ferraro
3. Three Mile Island
4. Boland Amendment
5. *perestroika, glasnost*
6. Robert Bork
7. Poland
8. Boris Yeltsin
9. Manuel Noriega
10. H. Ross Perot

Multiple Choice
1. c
2. d
3. b
4. a
5. c
6. c
7. a
8. b
9. d
10. d
11. b
12. b
13. a
14. c
15. b

Chapter 33

Matching A
1. c
2. d
3. b
4. a
5. f

Matching B
1. e
2. d
3. c
4. b
5. a

Completion
1. Sandra Day O'Connor
2. Phyllis Schlafly
3. sexual harrasment
4. Sunbelt
5. Asia, Latin America
6. education
7. melting pot
8. *Roe v. Wade*
9. gay liberation
10. illegal drugs

True/False
1. F
2. F
3. T
4. F
5. F
6. T
7. F
8. T
9. F
10. F

Multiple Choice
1. d
2. a
3. b
4. a
5. c
6. d
7. a
8. a
9. c
10. b
11. d
12. c
13. d
14. b
15. b